RAISING
UP A GENERATION OF
HEALTHY
THIRD
CULTURE
KIDS

A PRACTICAL GUIDE TO PREVENTIVE CARE

LAUREN WELLS

Raising Up a Generation of Healthy Third Culture Kids: A Practical Guide to Preventive Care
By Lauren Wells

Independently Published
Canby, OR
© 2020 Lauren Wells

Back cover photo by Jennifer Blair Photography
Cover design by Vanessa Mendozzi

ISBN 9798622212932

Edited by Deb Hall

"Lauren Wells begins her book by describing what she calls the "ampersand" life of the third culture kid, demonstrating the wonder, beauty, and difficulty of a global childhood. The description is remarkably accurate. If we could ensure that our TCKs would grow up healthy and resilient in this ampersand existence, able to withstand the inevitable adjustment process that comes with the global life and adapt accordingly, we would do it in a heartbeat. In Raising up a Generation of Healthy Third Culture Kids, Lauren Wells has gifted us with a gentle guide and a preventive health primer, unique in the field of third culture kid literature. As an adult third culture kid who works professionally as a public health nurse focused on prevention and wellness, I applaud the comprehensive content between these pages. The preventive wisdom in the book includes evidence-based practice around the adverse child events study and survey, research and findings from Dr. Brene Brown's work on belonging and fitting in, and important information from key thought leaders in the TCK world. It is a goldmine of wisdom, organized in a practical and readable format. While we cannot know all our TCKs will go through, we can take a giant step forward by reading this and learning how to multiply the benefits of a global life and conversely pay attention to the challenges that can become stumbling blocks to healthy development. If you are working with, raising, or love third culture kids from any part of the globe, buy this book today! The pages will quickly go from crisp and new to dogeared and underlined, worn in the best possible way for reading and internalizing this gift."

Marilyn Gardner
author of *Between Worlds: Essays on Culture and Belonging* and *Worlds Apart: A Third Culture Kid's Journey*

"With one foot firmly placed in the present, Lauren offers practical ideas for you and your family that you can implement today. But the real treasure of *Raising Up a Generation of Healthy Third Culture Kids* is that the other foot is equally firmly planted in the future. After working with hundreds of TCKS—and being one herself—Lauren wearied of addressing preventable parts of being a TCK with adult TCKs. Instead of doing clean-up work years after their childhood, she decided to equip parents and those who work with TCKS on how to address and process your life with your TCK. You and your family will grow closer, experience depth, and enjoy each other more after reading this book. If you do only one thing for your family this year, read this book."

Amy Young
author of *Looming Transitions and founder of Global Trellis*

"*Raising Up a Generation of Heathy Third Culture Kids* is a must-have for anyone currently or anticipating raising TCKs, adult TCKs seeking to make meaning of their extraordinary upbringing, and for practitioners working with TCKs and their families. Marrying new information on long-recognized challenges, Wells adds much needed insights. Her direct experience, research-informed knowledge, and skills-based expertise combine to make this a prevention-focused, resilience-enhancing classic you'll refer to - and recommend - often."

Linda A. Janssen
author *of The Emotionally Resilient Expat: Engage, Adapt and Thrive Across Cultures*

"Lauren has created an incredibly insightful and compassionate guide that concisely illuminates the TCK experience AND provides invaluable advice on how to raise TCKs well and thrive as a family. I found myself highlighting constantly as Lauren expertly translated complex ideas into easy to understand language with practical examples and guidance. This book doesn't just explain WHAT the TCK experience is, but HOW to truly cultivate it!"

Christopher O'Shaughnessy
author *of Arrivals, Departures and Adventures In-Between*

ACKNOWLEDGMENTS

Just one year ago, this book was barely an idea—one that I thought was crazy. Yet I am thankful for those who believed in, encouraged, pushed, and supported me to put my passion for preventive TCK care into writing.

Thank you, Heidi Tunberg, for being the first to teach me about Third Culture Kids and for being so patient and gentle as I processed through understanding that piece of my identity. You sparked my desire at fifteen years old to work one day with TCKs and their families.

Thank you to Linda Janssen, Jerry Jones, Chris O'Shaughnessy, Ruth Van Reken, and the CultureBound staff for being the first to nudge me to write a book.

Thank you, Tanya Crossman, for supporting me through this whole process and for gifting your writing talents to the foreword of this book.

Thank you to Margaret Bond, Tiffany Schlotter, Heather Brouhard, Nicole Bond, Cheri Shirley, James Amato, Cody Poor, Marilyn Gardner, Andrew Malm, Sarah Dodson, Craig Miller, Richard Alvarez, Chris Moyer, Bobbi Hall, Alyssa Brouhard, Tanya Crossman, Brian O'Connor, Terri Matthews, Amy Young, Kelly and Prissy Smith, Corrie Miller, Ace Brickman, Karen Wells, Tracie Reynolds Wright, Remy van den Bogaerdt, Kristen Robinson, Shannon Rants, Smitha Day, and the six who chose to remain anonymous for your contributions. I couldn't have done it without you.

Thank you, Jillian Alexander, for making me a better writer and keeping me company on long writing days.

Thank you to my amazing husband who has allowed me to take breaks from mom duty to go to a coffee shop to write for a couple of hours many a Saturday.

Thank you to my beautiful girls, Clara and Audrey, for teaching me daily how much I love (and know much less than I thought I did about) parenting.

Thank you to Deb Hall for your editing superpowers and your patience with my horrific endnotes.

Thank you to Mark Hedinger for your read-throughs, input, and constant encouragement throughout this whole process.

Finally, thank you to my wonderful parents, Tony and Holly Freitas, for moving us overseas. My life is what it is because of that decision and is the only reason why I could write this book.

Contents

FOREWORD

I have worked with and on behalf of TCKs for over 14 years now. I started out mentoring expatriate teenagers living in Beijing shortly after moving here myself as a young adult. After doing that for five or six years, I began to learn more about the plight of their parents. So many expatriate parents are weighed down by guilt and anxiety, fearing that by bringing their children overseas they have ruined their lives. Others are totally oblivious to ways they unintention- ally alienate their own children by failing to understand just how different this international upbringing is to how they themselves were raised.

I then wrote a book titled *"Misunderstood"* based on research I conducted to better understand TCKs. My point was not that TCKs will always be misunderstood, but to show that feeling misunder- stood is a significant negative experience for many – and one that can be mitigated when parents are willing to step in and learn how their children feel. The question is: knowing the issues many TCKs in the past have struggled with, are there things parents and other adults in their lives can do to help cushion them from potential problems in the future? I persist in the work I do because I believe the answer is an emphatic "yes!" *Raising Up a Generation of Healthy TCKs* is all about that emphatic yes: a book full of practical and easily applied strategies to offer preventive care to TCKs.

In a way, it feels like a sequel to my own book – a natural progression. When I wrote *Misunderstood*, my goal was to explain the perspective of TCKs to those who care for them. It has helped parents understand how their TCK children may be feeling, what they may be thinking, and how their perspective on life might differ from their parents'. It has helped ATCKs know they are not alone, giving a sense of validation and comfort. Those are really important steps! But many readers soon move on to a big question: what next? Now that they understand some of what an international childhood involves, what should they do about it? I am currently working on research to provide next steps for ATCKs. In *Raising Up a Generation of Healthy TCKs*, Lauren Wells provides a comprehensive answer for expat parents who are ready to act on behalf of their children.

Lauren tackles a selection of issues that are particularly important for TCKs generally, as children and as adults. She explains how these issues arise from an international childhood, and how they may influence a TCK's long term emotional and relational health. But most importantly, she then offers simple and practical strategies parents can immediately apply. There are examples, easy-to-follow instructions, and differing strategies for children at different ages or stages of life. There are also challenges for parents to work on their own emotional growth, so they can model healthy living to their children. In short, Lauren shows parents how to give their TCKs a strong foundation of emotional health as they move toward adulthood.

As I speak to parents, educators, and TCKs themselves around the world I field the same questions over and over. I share practical tools and strategies in my seminars, but until now there was a definite gap in the resources I could recommend for parents to work on at home. This book fills that gap perfectly.

I love that *Raising Up a Generation of Healthy TCKs* exists, because I now have the perfect resource to recommend to every parent looking for ways to help their TCK children.

Tanya Crossman
Author of *Misunderstood: The Impact of Growing Up Overseas in the 21st Century*

INTRODUCTION

I love the ampersand (&) as a depiction of the Third Culture Kid (TCK) life. It is a great symbol of the both/and nature of life at times and has been the best way I have found to answer the question, "What was it like to grow up overseas?" It was an ampersand, a both/and. It was both wonderful and difficult, both joy filled and grief filled, both so good and so hard. For each challenge, there was a contrasting benefit that could be birthed out of the difficulty.

My family began traversing the globe when my mom started working for a mission organization in California when I was seven years old. She would routinely go on international work trips and bring home exotic gifts and spices that she would use to recreate the ethnic foods that she had tried. I went on a trip with her for the first time at ten years old to Ethiopia, Kenya, and Tanzania. I fell in love with Africa during those four weeks, so a couple of years later, when I was twelve years old and my parents announced that we would be moving to Tanzania, I was thrilled.

The years in Africa that would follow were exactly the ampersand life that I described. I learned to speak Swahili, to cook Tanzanian food, and I had the freedom to run around the village because everyone kept an eye out for each other's kids. It was the prime environment for my independent nature. My younger brother and I raised baby hedgehogs and pet monkeys and routinely rescued stray puppies. I hiked with friends in a gorge filled with giant waterfalls, rainbows, and butterflies. We camped often—once in the Serengeti listening to lions walking around our tents and hyenas laughing in the distance, another time in the bush at the foot of an erupting, glowing volcano. I often slept on cowhides in a Maasai village eight hours from the nearest town. With the light pollution equally as far away, many hours were spent lying on the roof of our Land Rover counting dozens of shooting stars. Safaris became normal, and so did eating weevils in our oatmeal. It was incredible.

AND (&)...people close to me died of HIV/AIDS, I witnessed murders, and our home was robbed. I struggled to find a sense of belonging, to process grief and loss, to make friends after saying constant good-byes. As an adult I didn't know how to stay in one place for longer than a year, to develop deep relationships with people or places, how to work though unresolved grief and the anxiety that resulted. I battled night terrors and fears of never being truly understood. My life overseas was certainly incredible & it was certainly hard.

By sharing this book, I hope to provide a practical resource and guide for how to maximize the benefits and decrease the negative effects of the many challenges of raising kids in another culture. In essence, I hope to address both sides of the ampersand. In my experience working in this field for the past several years and being in the globally mobile world most of my life, I've noticed that people tend to focus on one side or the other—pointing out all the challenges from a fairly hopeless perspective, or not acknowledging that the challenges exist and only promoting the benefits. Having lived this ampersand life, I know that the experience is not at all black-and-white. It is a complex array of blended colors that include just as many complex emotions.

I write this book from a place of hope. I believe that we can raise healthy kids outside their passport countries and that these kids can grow up to be incredible contributors to our world. I also believe that we need to take seriously the challenges that so many face because of their unique lifestyles and be proactive about preventive care for Third Culture Kids. I am not a parenting expert. I even cringe at being called a TCK expert. Can anyone really be an expert at anything that involves human beings? We can research, understand, and learn to better navigate things like parenting, but since the beginning of time, no one has created the perfect parenting formula and I certainly am not going to attempt to do so now. But I have seen the TCK road map and walked for a while down the rocky trail—first on my own and then holding the hands of hundreds of families who are braving the same journey. I trust and hope that my experience will be valuable to those who are traversing the same path. This book is filled with practical, encouraging, and easy-to-implement ideas that I pray give you a sense of hope and direction as you love and support your Third Culture Kids throughout their ampersand lives.

DEFINITIONS

It is important that we understand the definition of Third Culture Kids and the wider context that they fall into. The most commonly accepted definitions are those developed by Ruth Van Reken and Michael Pollock and, though the general definitions have not changed, they have been revised over the years and I'll be using the most current in this book.

CROSS-CULTURAL KIDS

Third Culture Kids fall into a broader category called Cross-Cultural Kids.

"A Cross-Cultural Kid is a person who has lived in-or meaningfully interacted with two or more cultural environments for a significant period of time during developmental years."[1]

Examples of Cross-Cultural Kids include:

- traditional TCKs,
- bi/multi-cultural and/or bi/multi-racial children,
- children of immigrants,
- children of refugees,
- children of minorities,
- international adoptees,
- domestic TCKs (those who live in a subculture within their passport culture).

For the purpose of this book, we will focus on Traditional TCKs because the challenges and benefits show up in their most extreme form in the Traditional TCK population. However, if you are raising, working with, or loving on kids who fit into the overall CCK category, know that much of what is covered in this book will apply to them as well.

THIRD CULTURE KIDS

A traditional Third Culture Kid (TCK) is a person who spends a significant part of his or her first eighteen years of life accompanying parents into a country that is different from at least one parent's passport country(ies) due to a parent's choice of work or advanced training.[2]

Mission organizations, universities, international businesses, governmental institutions, and parents all around the world are taking a deeper look into the growing people group known as Third Culture Kids (TCKs) because the growth of the global TCK population is so rapid.

This growth is due to people all around the world moving out of their passport countries at enormous rates—more than any other time in history—and raising their children in new cultures. According to a recent report from the United Nations, "the number of international migrants globally reached an estimated 272 million in 2019, an increase of 51 million since 2010. Currently, international migrants comprise 3.5 per cent of the global population, compared to 2.8 per cent in the year 2000."[3]

In 1989 sociologist Dr. Ted Ward predicted that "Third Culture Kids would be the prototype citizens of the future."[4] Therapist Lois Bushong said, "What Dr. Ward meant was that in today's globalizing world, more and more people would grow up among many cultural worlds even if they didn't move overseas with their parents. Even those who never moved very far geographically would see the world coming to them. Ultimately, a cross-cultural childhood is becoming the new normal all across the globe for virtually everyone."[5]

This phenomenon of rapid globalization has a direct impact on our society and the world as a whole. We have never before experienced such an intermixed population, but we do know a considerable amount about what that could look like because of the research done on the TCK population. Unfortunately, the research shows that while there are many benefits to growing up globally, TCKs are also prone to many challenges. As with any upbringing, however, there are ways to be proactive about preventing negative manifestations of those challenges and maximizing the incredible benefits these global citizens can have. And the effect is farther reaching than your own home and family. By addressing and preventing the known challenges and helping TCKs reap the benefits of this lifestyle, we are also proactively helping the world to learn to navigate this new multicultural norm.

COMMON CHALLENGES AND BENEFITS OF THE TCK LIFE

GRIEF

Third Culture Kids are guaranteed to experience a considerable amount of grief and loss during their developmental years. These losses come in the form of relationships, places, identity, community, etc., and for most TCKs these losses compound and go unacknowledged. This can lead to the common TCK challenge of unresolved grief.

TRAUMA

TCKs also experience more trauma than the average person. They are more likely to be affected by complex trauma (involving a series of repeated stressful events), extreme trauma, and often high exposure to traumatic situations. This is especially true when living in a Third World country.

IDENTITY AND BELONGING

Thirty-three percent of TCKs report feeling misunderstood by their parents, 41 percent by friends in their host countries, and 67 percent by friends in their passport countries.[6] Most TCKs struggle with a lack of belonging. They don't feel that they fit completely in their passport countries, their host countries, and perhaps even in their immediate families. They struggle to figure out who they are in the midst of all the adapting that they do, and they often have ties to many different communities which leaves them wondering if they fully belong in any of them.

NEED FOR CHANGE

Feeling settled is often an uncomfortable feeling for TCKs. Thus, many have a mental alarm clock that goes off every couple of years that urges them to start over with new people, new places, new things. This need for change may be present in childhood and adolescence, but more commonly arises and causes difficulty in adulthood when settling becomes the societal expectation.

RELATIONSHIP STRUGGLES

Third Culture Kids often struggle in adulthood to have deep, meaningful relationships. They are very good at the initial interaction and the beginning stages of a relationship, but once it gets beyond a certain point, they lose interest and move on to a new set of friendships. This challenge in navigating relationships can be the core cause of many other issues since meaningful relationships are critical to one's health and well-being.

SUBCONSCIOUS EXPECTATIONS

Living a unique life sets TCKs up with many interesting expectations of what a "normal" life looks like. This can be detrimental when they grow into adulthood and find that they are unable to replicate the incredible experiences that they grew up with or achieve the high standards that they always seemed to as a child. Combatting these expectations becomes an important part of raising healthy TCKs.

SHAME

TCKs are prone to deep-seated shame when they enter adulthood because of their inability to fit in as intuitively as everyone else. They are incredibly good at looking like they fit in, and thus, the shame says, "You can't fool everyone forever. You don't really belong. If they knew what was behind your mask, they would reject you." This hidden shame too often becomes a recipe for lack of relationship, which leads to isolation—the primary source of depression.[7]

Each of these challenges, if unaddressed, can lead to mental health issues, relationship issues, and many other serious challenges. If we know that most TCKs and CCKs deal with these challenges in some form, then we have to think about what will happen when the majority of the world's children are CCKs or TCKs. How can we prevent these issues from negatively affecting the next generation?

The good news: we have a prototype! Let's find ways to prevent these issues from becoming debilitating in the next generation of TCKs and CCKs and thus help them reap the incredible benefits of a cross-cultural upbringing.

BENEFITS OF THE TCK EXPERIENCE

- Remarkable adaptation abilities
- Global citizenship that yields an expanded worldview
- Exceptionally high achievers and "outside the box" thinkers
- Unique and intuitive ability to empathize
- Language skills
- High emotional intelligence
- Early independence and maturity

Thinking about current events in the world right now involving racism, immigration, war, natural disasters, political strife, and the like, it is clear how TCKs and CCKs can be an incredible asset to our world. As our world becomes increasingly more integrated, it will be the adult TCKs and CCKs who can truly help navigate this new globalized society. If we focus now on finding ways to raise healthy TCKs and CCKs, we are well on our way to seeing the coming generation make some incredible changes in our world because of their cross-cultural upbringing.

My goal for this book is to offer practical skills for anyone who loves and supports TCKs and globally mobile families. To empower and equip parents, organizations, teachers, grandparents, international schools, anyone who has TCKs in their life with an understanding of preventive TCK care, and how to implement it so that they can live a healthier life both during their developmental years overseas and in adulthood.

Anytime I read a book or article that presents a theory, I think, "That's great, but what do I do with it?" This book is the answer to that question.

The theory: "Being proactive about the way we care for TCKs

can help them to live a healthy life both as children and adults."

This book: "Here's how you do that in practical ways."

I hope that this book turns into the handbook that you will open so many times that the insides start falling out, the margins get all scribbled in, the pages all get dog-eared, and you've gifted copies to all the globally mobile families in your life.

CHAPTER 1

Understanding the Need for Preventive Care

Healthy TCKs have been preventively cared for throughout their lives and thus possess benefits that have been intentionally and lovingly mined out of each challenge.

Prevention science is a field that is rapidly increasing in popularity as more and more people rally around the mantra "prevention is always better than a cure." In my work with globally mobile families, I have found this to be profoundly true. We know that moving overseas with children provides them with an incredible opportunity for wonderful and unique benefits. We also know that their cross-cultural upbringing makes them susceptible to many challenges that often manifest in their adult lives. An increasing number of resources are available for these adults who need the support and services to counteract the challenges they are facing, and this is absolutely wonderful. My goal, in contrast, is to start on the other end—to begin supporting families while their children are young and to apply practical prevention science to globally mobile families like yours with the hope that it will decrease the risks and increase the benefits of the TCK life.

WHAT EXACTLY ARE WE PREVENTING?

The challenges that TCKs face because of their upbringing cannot be prevented. They are a part of the package that comes with choosing to live the globally mobile life. However, when the challenges are managed throughout the TCK's life, we are preventing those challenges from manifesting in adulthood as mental illness, relationship issues, and inability to live a healthy lifestyle.

Based on recent research we know that

- 90 percent of TCKs say they are more or less "out of synch" with their age group throughout their lifetime;[8]
- expatriates experience 2.5 times higher rates of mental illness than the general population;
- three times as many expatriates report feeling trapped and depressed than monocultural individuals;
- more than 50 percent of expatriates self-report internalizing disorders such as anxiety disorders and depression;[9]
- depression and suicide rates are more prominent among TCKs.[10]

While there is relatively little published research on the mental health of adult TCKs, new research studies are predicting the rates for depression and anxiety in adult TCKs are upwards of 80 percent. There are, however, many more research studies on expatriate families as a whole and show that parents of TCKs often struggle significantly (2.5 times higher rates of mental illness) while living overseas. Because we know that the health of the parents directly correlates with the health of the children, we can factor in those statistics and deduce that their children may be negatively affected and that this correlates with the findings we are beginning to see in the research on adult TCKs. I believe that the proactive techniques that you'll learn throughout these pages, if implemented, will be beneficial for the health of the entire family.

OTHER FACTORS AFFECTING TCK HEALTH

What is the root cause of the challenges we are seeing in adult TCKs? What could be the scientific reason for extremely high rates of anxiety, depression, and other serious issues? In recent years, researchers have found surprising links between childhood experiences and health in adulthood – both physical and mental. Two of these that I believe apply directly to the TCK experience are toxic stress and ACE scores.

TOXIC STRESS

Toxic stress often occurs in the life of expatriate children. Many of us in the TCK world refer to this phenomenon as "Expat Child Syndrome" and use this term to explain the emotional, behavioral, and/or physical challenges that many TCKs struggle with, particularly during periods of transition. Kelli Harding explains in The Rabbit Effect, "Toxic stress [in children] can result from strong, frequent, or prolonged activation of the body's stress response systems in the absence of the buffering protection of a supportive, adult relationship."[11] Because it is during their formative years that TCKs are transitioning between cultures and living cross-culturally, they are susceptible to experiencing intense stress, and because their parents are often also experiencing intense stress, they may not offer the "buffering protection" that they perhaps would in a more settled life. Research has shown us that toxic or prolonged stress during childhood "increases inflammation, shortens telomeres, and alters epigenetics, which puts a person at risk of heart attack, stroke, infection, cancer, diabetes, mental illnesses, osteoporosis, autoimmune disorders, and premature death." However, the contrary is also true. When we can combat toxic stress and thus lower our (or our kids') stress levels, we are healthier in general and even recover faster when we do experience disease.[12]

ACE SCORES

I have heard the argument many times that children are resilient, but I beg to differ and so does the research. Dr. Felitti, along with the Center for Disease Control (CDC), designed and performed a large-scale study to determine just how closely our childhood experiences are tied to our health as adults.[13] The study asked ten "yes" or "no" questions about exposure to negative childhood events such as substance abuse in the home, a mentally ill parent, and separated or divorced parents. The number of "yes" answers determined the respondent's ACE (Adverse Childhood Experience) score. This extensive work showed that the number of an individual's ACE score directly and drastically influenced his or her health as an adult. The more negative (or adverse) experiences we have in childhood, the more likely we are to become unhealthy adults. Here is a clear example: "Compared with someone who has an ACE score of zero, a person with an ACE score of 4 or more is twice as likely to have heart disease and cancer, seven times more likely to be addicted to alcohol and 12 times more likely to attempt suicide."[14] You can learn more about ACE scores and determine your own at www. ACEsTooHigh.com.

I do not write this to suggest that your TCK necessarily has a high ACE score or has suffered from toxic stress, but I do want to show that there is a direct influence between a child's experiences during their developmental years and their health later in life. We also know that because of the unique lifestyle of expatriate families, TCKs are prone to experiencing toxic stress and increased ACE Scores. In a study done on toxic stress in children, it was found that a supportive, adult relationship is the key to combatting the body's stress response system that keeps the stress from being toxic. By being aware of the stressors that are prevalent in the TCK life and learning tools for prevention, you are more equipped to be that supportive relationship for your TCKs.

WHAT IS THE GOAL?

If we successfully prevent toxic stress and high ACE scores, what then is the outcome? What does a healthy TCK look like? Certainly, we are unable to keep them from experiencing difficulty, and we know that through trials great traits like resilience and empathy are born. We are not expecting that their adult lives will be storybook perfect, nor are we assuming that if we simply apply the right formula, they will live successful lives. So, what do I mean by "healthy TCKs"?

Healthy TCKs:

- have been preventively cared for throughout their lives and thus possess benefits that have been intentionally and loving mined out of each challenge;
- know how to feel and process a full range of emotions in a

constructive and fruitful way and thus, become a model of emotional intelligence;

- are in-tune to the emotional needs of others because they have either had their needs met by intentional, engaging, healthy parents during their developmental years, or they have processed and grieved the pain of unmet needs;
- allow themselves to love people and places enough to feel the pain of each loss and give themselves permission to grieve each time they leave or are left;
- have processed the grief of their TCK experience and know how to work through difficult emotions in a healthy and productive way;
- feel, process, and resolve their grief and through it develop a beautiful ability for empathy, connection, and compassion;
- have addressed and processed the difficulties of their TCK lives and reaped a beautiful resiliency as a result;
- have pieces of their identity that remain anchored while they skillfully adapt to the cultures around them;
- accept that they are a blend of cultures and places and can claim, and relish in, an integrated life;
- have learned to develop and maintain deep relationships that have spanned multiple seasons of their adult life;
- have learned how to control the need for change instead of letting it control them, know how to combat their restlessness in healthy ways, and allow themselves to be "settled" in the necessary areas of life;
- are able to be vulnerable by lifting their mask and showing who they uniquely are, not the perfect version for the culture they are surrounded by, and recognize that this is not a

shameful act but, on the contrary, is incredibly brave;

- are aware of their subconscious expectations of life and of themselves and have learned to offer themselves grace for their imperfections and develop contentment in their lifestyle;
- have recognized and processed the challenges of their unique upbringing and live out the benefits in their own life, recognizing that they are directly attributed to, and are often a product of, their TCK experience.

Of course, there will never be a point when a TCK has "arrived" and has no more room to grow in these areas. We are all constantly growing, changing, and learning. But, it is important that we know what we are aiming for personally as TCKs and for you, parents and caregivers, to know what it looks like to be on the flip-side of each of the TCK challenges that we'll talk about. This changes the perspective. Instead of seeing the TCK-life as full of horrible potential issues to prevent, we can look at this list and see the amazing benefits to attain to. I believe this is a much healthier and more hope-filled approach.

WHERE TO BEGIN

Prevention can include a variety of elements, but I have specifically identified seven that families can focus on. The first two, pre-field training and education, can be helpful ways of gaining understanding, preparation, and ongoing support for the overseas experience. The final four spell out the acronym CARE (Conversations, Awareness, Relationship, and Example). These four prevention elements are what we will focus on throughout this book and I hope will be applied throughout your entire experience of raising Third Culture Kids.

PRE-FIELD TRAINING

We know that people who receive training before they move overseas are more likely to be successful on the field. This is especially true for families with children. I believe that one of the best ways to prepare children for the TCK life is to equip them with skills for learning a new culture and language and for navigating transition. I work as the Director of Training for an organization called Culture-Bound, and in 2015 I developed their pre-field training programs for children and teens. It has been amazing to see the transformation in kids when they realize that they too can have a toolbox of ways to learn culture and language when they move overseas. They feel a sense of purpose instead of feeling like they are just tagging along with their parents, and they have a foundational knowledge of the TCK life that they are entering into. Pre-field training is a great starting place for preventive care.

EDUCATION

Parent workshops on raising TCKs are also incredibly important as you move overseas with kids. Developing an awareness of the issues, trends, and strategic ways to implement preventive care and having a place to ask questions and dive into your family's specific situation can more fully prepare you as you begin the journey of raising TCKs. After teaching one of these workshops, I had a mother say to me, "We have had so much training but nothing that spoke to our hearts like what you have taught us about our children. What we have learned will be life changing for us and for them."

I regularly offer online workshops through my organization TCK Training (www.TCKTraining.com). During these workshops, parents and those who work with TCKs can expand on the concepts in this book in an interactive way. We learn from each other through discussion and hear about different ways preventive TCK care is being implemented.

EVERYDAY CARE

The acronym CARE stands for Conversations, Awareness, Relationship, and Example. This everyday CARE is where this book comes in. You are a critical part of raising healthy TCKs, and it is in the everyday normal life moments that you are molding and shaping your TCKs. By being aware of the challenges they face, having age-appropriate conversations with them, developing deep relationships with your TCKs, and modeling healthy behavior, you are setting them up for success as adults.

C – Conversations

Sometimes it can be overwhelming to think about how to talk to your children about difficult things in a healthy and understandable way. I often find that when I hear parenting advice that recommends I should talk to my toddlers about such and such, I find myself thinking, "That sounds great, but what do I *actually* say?" In the following chapters I give tangible conversation guides and ideas for talking with your TCKs at every age about complex subjects in a simplified way.

A – Awareness

I wish my parents would have known the challenges that TCKs come up against in the overseas life. They had no training, no mentors who had gone before, no awareness of the TCK experience. This was unfortunately the norm until more recent years when the TCK concept became more widely taught and understood. Still, there are many who, though they know *what* a TCK is, don't know the extent to which TCKs struggle with various issues, nor do they have a picture of what a healthy adult TCK can look like. Parents who are living or are about to live overseas with their children need to be aware of the challenges of the TCK life and how those challenges manifest if they are not addressed. Often the challenges are not outwardly noticeable in childhood, especially early childhood, so parents don't see a clear need for managing, or even having, a conversation about these challenges. But what we know about the TCK life is that all these challenges that occur in childhood are likely to have long-term ramifications in adulthood if they are not tended to *before* they become obvious issues. When parents are aware of the complexities, breadth, and depth of the issues they can pro-actively implement skills, tools, and strategies as they raise their TCKs. I hope that your sense of awareness shifts dramatically by the time you finish reading this book.

R – Relationship

Parent-child relationships are the most foundational relationships we have as humans, and this becomes even more extreme for parents and children who enter the globally mobile life. Often the members of the nuclear family are the only people who have been together through the same experiences. This shared experience is, for many TCKs, something that will only ever be between them and their parents and siblings. For this reason, parents are the primary influencers in raising healthy TCKs. This relationship should be highly upheld, protected, and cherished. TCKs need to know that their parents are one thing that remains stable in their ever-changing world, and that stability is only felt in relationship.

E – Example

Researcher Dr. Brené Brown says, "Who we are and how we engage with the world are much stronger predictors of how our children will do than what we know about parenting."[15] Child development research has taught us that children learn considerably more from watching their parents model behavior than through what is spoken because of neurons in our brain called mirror neurons. These neurons fire in your child's brain when they are watching you do something in the same way that they are firing in your brain as you actually do it. When we as parents respond to stressful or frightening situations, we imprint that response into our children's mirror neurons. Later in life they will likely automatically respond to the same stimuli and situations in the same way that they saw us respond.[16]

Mirror neurons are particularly active when it comes to more complex elements like emotional regulation and expression, relationship dynamics, and conflict resolution. It is interesting because these are also most often the things that parents try to avoid their children seeing. We often don't want our children to see us cry or work through anger or carry out healthy conflict resolution. If our children see us cry, we paint on a smile and say things like, "Mommy is okay! No need to worry about me!" And we talk out our marital conflicts behind closed doors. There are certainly times when this is appropriate, but somehow children, especially TCKs, need to see an example of how to do these things in healthy ways.

This modeling is particularly important for TCKs because the various cultures around them may each be doing things differently. You can provide clarity for the inevitable confusion by exhibiting healthy behaviors for your children. For most TCKs the members of the nuclear family are the only people in the world who have been there with them through all the transitions, new places, new cultures, new languages, and new people during their developmental years. This means that, for many TCKs, parents are the only consistent example in their lives. Parents model how to – or how not to - transition from one place to another in a healthy way, process grief and other difficult emotions, develop a healthy identity, and foster healthy relationships. We'll talk about each of these throughout this book and how you can be a model of health in these areas. Unlike monocultural children who likely have consistent people in their lives outside their nuclear families, TCKs rarely see people other than their immediate family members live through various life seasons. This is why this idea of being an example and modeling for your TCKs is critically important—they need you to be their model because you may be the only consistent example they have.

RELATED BENEFITS:

Each chapter of this book will end with the related benefits associated with the challenges discussed in the chapter. The final chapter will look at each of those in more depth and how to encourage them. Again, my goal is for you to feel hopeful as you read each chapter.

While we will be discussing difficult realities of the TCK life, it is so important to also look at the benefits that can only come from walking through those challenges.

THE MAIN IDEAS:

- We have to be preventive in our approach to TCK care if we have any hope of raising up a generation of healthy TCKs.
- Pre-field training and education for both parents and children are important prevention tools.
- C – Conversations
  A – Awareness
  R – Relationship
  E – Example

CAREing for your TCK by having conversations about all aspects of the TCK life, developing awareness about the intricacies of the TCK life, strengthening your relationship with your TCK, and modeling a healthy lifestyle through example is critical to their long-term health.

QUESTIONS TO CONSIDER:

- How does it make you feel to read about toxic stress, ACE scores, and their relationship to TCKs?
- How important do you believe preventive care is for your TCK(s)?
- What is an action step you plan to take from this chapter?

CHAPTER 2

Laying the Groundwork for Healthy Third Culture Kids

Healthy TCKs know how to feel and process a full range of emotions in a constructive and fruitful way and thus, become a model of emotional intelligence.

P arents and others who love and support TCKs are in a prime position to build a healthy foundation for TCKs as they grow so that they have a solid platform from which to jump into their adult lives. This book will explore several specific ways that parents and caregivers can build this foundation for each specific challenge. However, there are a few elements that underline this foundation. The concepts and practices we will cover in this chapter become the underlying framework for the other skills that we'll look at in later chapters.

BUILDING THE EMOTIONAL FOUNDATION

The primary source of foundation building for your children is your presence.

The parent-child relationship is the most crucial relationship we have as human beings. When that relationship is healthy, children are more likely to grow into stable, healthy adults who are less likely to deal with issues such as body dissatisfaction (particularly girls), low self-esteem, and depression.[17]

Your relationship with your children also teaches them from the day they are born how relationships work. When they see you reacting to their cries, smiles, questions, and mistakes, it shows them what they can and should expect from any relationship.[18] This is one reason why it is particularly important that families who live overseas are conscious of their relationships with their TCKs. Expatriate families often experience high levels of stress and anxiety, particularly during times of transition. It is during these high-intensity seasons that your relationship with your TCKs become a direct influence on how they process these situations themselves.[19] While it is difficult in the midst of your own fear and anxiety, it is in this space that your TCKs need to be pulled in extra close to you in order to feel safe and secure in your relationships with them. "A child's ability to gain self-confidence is fundamentally relational and based on the safe relationship she has with loving parents, particularly when she's in stressful situations."[20]

Not only is the parent-child relationship critical for TCKs, but its impact continues beyond that. Parenting expert Dr. Joshua Straub says about his own parenting, "The quality of my presence while they're under my roof will one day determine the quality of their presence under their own."[21] It is through being present and engaging with your TCKs that you are truly able to build a healthy emotional foundation, and by building this emotional foundation, you are setting them up to do the same for their own children one day.

While this idea of a healthy parent-child relationship seems good in theory, if you are a parent, you know that your relationships with your children are not always picture-perfect. We are imperfect beings, and thus, misunderstandings, arguments, and breakdowns in communication are inevitable. But, as Dr. Daniel Siegel says, "The key is to repair any breach as quickly as possible—and it's our responsibility as parents to initiate this. When we reconnect with our kids, we model a crucial skill that will allow them to enjoy much more meaningful relationships as they grow up."[22] Because TCKs often develop a habit of breaking off relationships instead of repairing them when a difficulty arises, this is an important skill for them to learn.

To learn more about healthy parent-child relationships, I highly recommend the book *Safe House* by Dr. Joshua Straub. In it he says, "Kids who develop a secure relationship with their parent in a safe environment are more likely able to:

- Experience and label a wide range of emotions, from positive to negative
- Balance and regulate these emotions, especially intense ones
- Learn how to manage and lessen fear
- Develop insight into and understanding of their own thoughts, feelings, and behavior
- Be more aware of how others are feeling in a given situation and respond to their felt needs
- Empathize with others
- Have a deeper understanding of the difference between right and wrong."[23]

You can see from this list why your relationships with your TCKs are the most fundamental foundation-building aspect of raising healthy TCKs. While I hope to give you a plethora of helpful ideas throughout this book, not one will be effective without a healthy parent-child relationship.

PRACTICE USING FEELING WORDS

Emotional health is severely lacking in the TCK world. The primary cause is a lack of permission to recognize, verbalize, and experience all emotions. Most TCKs feel as if they are living life in a fishbowl, so to speak, and that the expectation of the onlookers is that they should be happily, gratefully, and blissfully swimming around and loving their lives. They grow to be afraid not only to express negative thoughts or emotions but also even to feel them. This not only creates the obvious problem of lack of emotional processing (which leads to a host of other problems that we will discuss in chapter 5 on grief) but also causes them not to talk about anything that could be negative. This keeps trauma, grief, shame, and so many other issues from being processed and resolved, and when this happens, a breeding ground is created for so many debilitating challenges for TCKs to grow.

One way to begin developing their emotional health is by teaching them to recognize, feel, and name their emotions. This not only helps them as they navigate the challenges of the TCK life, but it is arguably the most critical factor in any child's success and well-being as an adult, TCK or not. Because of your unique family life, you have a great opportunity to foster this skill very intentionally.

One of the easiest ways to begin teaching your kids to recognize, feel, and name their feelings is by introducing a feelings chart. You can find great options through Google ("Kids Emotion Chart") or by visiting the worksheets page on my website (www.TCKTraining.com). The charts are simply a visual tool for learning to identify a wide variety of emotions. Print a few copies, laminate or cover them with clear tape if possible, and keep them in different places that you frequent: the dining room table, the car, your child's room, etc. Try to refer to them frequently.

For example, when you pick up your child from school, refer to the feelings chart and say to him or her, "How was your school day? Can you show me a face that looks like how you felt at school today?"

Because kids are kids, they will often choose something silly or not give a serious answer. That is okay! Allow them to do so. They are still looking at the different emotions, expressions, and imagining that feeling as they speak to you about it. The idea is not always to get deep inside their emotional worlds but instead to start giving them a well-developed vocabulary of emotions and for them to begin mentally connecting feeling words to events. When they are genuinely going through a difficult season or experience, they will have a large pool of words to use to express to you or other trusted people, and more importantly to themselves, how they are feeling.

GIVE PERMISSION TO FEEL

The TCK life presents an array of difficult emotions, which often feel off-limits to TCKs and even their parents. Because the overseas life is filled with so much excitement and is surrounded by so much good and so many unique experiences, it can seem like acknowledging negative emotions means being ungrateful for the amazing life you live or exaggerating the difficulties. This is a common pitfall for TCKs and is often the root of unresolved grief and trauma. Like the ampersand idea I suggested at the outset of this book, something can be so good and so hard at the same time. To talk only about the good and not acknowledge the hard stunts the TCK's emotional maturity, self-awareness, and overall health. TCKs need special, consistent permission to feel negative feelings.

The emotions chart that I discussed is a great way to show them that they have permission to experience all emotions. Perhaps even reiterate that none of the emotions on the chart are off-limits—they can choose any of them. However, there are appropriate ways to express emotions. A great way to emphasize this to your TCK is by responding to inappropriate behavior by saying, "You are allowed to feel _____, but in our family, we don't _____ when we're feeling _____. Instead you can _____." This method makes it clear that the emotion is allowed, encourages a sense of family identity (which we'll discuss more in chapter 7), and provides an option for appropriately dealing with that emotion. For most children this needs to involve something physical. For example, "You are allowed to feel angry, but in our family, we don't throw things when we're feeling angry. Instead, why don't we go outside and play."

NARRATE YOUR CHILD'S FEELINGS

I have found that my three-year-old does better in unfamiliar situations when I narrate for her. When we are on our way to whatever activity it is, I explain, to the best of my ability, what she can expect and what I expect of her.

When I talked with TCK counselor Josh Sandoz, he mentioned the idea of not just narrating expectations, but, more importantly, narrating your child's feelings. This is particularly useful when you are moving overseas and entering a land of many unknowns. Young children have not yet learned to reason through their thoughts and feelings, so when they are overwhelmed by them, they can act out or shut down. I have seen many parents surprised at how severely or uncharacteristically their child reacts during the transition period of moving overseas. Sometimes these behaviors last well into the first year in the new culture or even beyond. Narrating your child's feelings is one way to help them work through the challenges that they don't have the words or maturity to work through on their own, and it combats their natural response to act out or shut down.

What does narrating emotions look like? Below are a few examples.

Example 1:
"Wow! That was a really long flight, and I'm sure you are very tired. I'm feeling a bit grumpy because I'm so tired, but I bet when we sit down and get some food, we will all feel better. How are you feeling, son?"

Example 2:
"Your new school will probably be very different from your old school, and that might make you feel a bit anxious and uncomfortable. After you have been there for a while, it will probably start to feel more normal, but it is okay not to love it right away."

Example 3:
"When we go to the market, there will probably be a lot of people, and because you have light skin and hair, they may touch you. I know that it makes you feel mad when people you don't know touch you, so when you start to feel that, squeeze my hand and we'll find

a place to go and take a little break."

Here are some things to keep in mind while narrating emotions:

Choose small, digestible feeling words that your children can grasp. Over time their feeling word vocabulary will expand with the use of your emotions chart, but when you are using narration in already potentially overwhelming situations, stick to words that they already know. When they are in more comfortable, predictable situations, look for ways to narrate to expand their feeling word vocabulary. If you do this regularly, you will have a larger word pool to pull from when you're in more challenging situations.

Don't assume that you know what your child is feeling. For very young children, you may need to tell them what they might be feeling (see Examples 2 and 3 above), but with older children, take the time to ask them how they feel in a particular situation. In this scenario, narrating might be describing your own feelings to normalize those feelings for your child (see Example 1).

Give them permission to feel. Narrating should normalize and validate feelings, not tell them why they should or shouldn't feel a certain way. Look at Example 2. In the example, the child's feeling is acknowledged and validated, and he or she is given permission to feel negative feelings. It can be tempting to say instead, "Your new school will probably be very different from your old school, and that might make you feel a bit anxious and uncomfortable, but there's no reason to feel that way! You're going to love it in no time!" While this example may seem harmlessly optimistic, it communicates to your child that they are not allowed or don't have a valid reason to feel anxious and uncomfortable. This not only doesn't take away their negative emotions but may also keep them from sharing them with you in the future.

Provide a solution. See Example 3. The parent foresees that the child may encounter a situation that may be a trigger for anger, but instead of saying, "Don't get angry" (which may be difficult or impossible for a child to control and also isn't healthy), give them a solution ("When you start to feel angry, squeeze my hand and we'll find a place to go and take a little break.") This teaches them to work through their negative emotions in healthy ways—a practice that has lifelong benefits.

The purpose of doing this emotional narrating is to normalize and validate your child's feelings, give them an appropriate way to work through those feelings, and show them that you experience uncomfortable and overwhelming feelings as well. While you may not be able to predict what every situation will look like (especially when you are in an unfamiliar culture yourself!), you do know a lot about your child and may be able to anticipate what negative emotional triggers they might encounter. Not only will this help your child, but you may find that this practice helps you to expand your own self-awareness and adaptability, creating an even greater sense of security for your child.

FAMILY CHECK-INS

The idea of family debriefs was introduced to me several years ago by cross-cultural consulting expert Libby Stephens. Any time I work with parents, I introduce this idea because I believe it plays a key role in preventive care. I call them "family check-ins."

Begin now the practice of having a family check-in each night. This can take place around the dinner table, at bedtime, or at any other time of the day when the family is all together.

During family check-ins:

- Use your emotions chart to ask each family member to point to how they are feeling at that moment and why.
- Go around the group and have each family member answer the questions, "What was the best part of your day?" and "What was the hardest part of your day?"
- When you hear the answers, be cognizant not to discredit their answers but instead ask questions to explore why something felt the "best" or "hardest" to them.
- Create an environment where each person can talk without being interrupted.
- Parents, give genuine answers. Kids need to hear that parents have "highs and lows" as well, and it is often through the parents' answers that using the feelings chart is clearly modeled. It is okay if your children give silly answers, but make sure you are giving honest ones to provide an example for them.

The reason for these family check-ins goes far beyond having a simple discussion. This practice puts into place a debriefing process so that when challenging things take place during your time overseas, there is already a routine in place that allows the family members to process together each day. This prevents it from being an awkward new thing when something difficult happens. When your family is familiar with the check-in system, familiar sharing feelings with each other, and familiar talking about difficult aspects of the day, it becomes the perfect environment for processing challenging experiences or crises.

Family check-in time can also be a great time to implement many of the skills that will be discussed in the chapters to come. You'll be able to use this time to practice intentionally using unfamiliar tools and having guided conversations.

RELATED BENEFITS — EMOTIONAL INTELLIGENCE:

TCKs have the capacity to be very emotionally intelligent individuals because of the spectrum of life events they live through during their developmental years. When they learn to name, express, and process their feelings, they develop a mature emotional vocabulary and emotional intelligence. Emotional Intelligence is "the ability to identify and name one's own emotions; the ability to harness those emotions and apply them to tasks like thinking and problem solving; and the ability to manage emotions, which includes both regulating one's own emotions when necessary and helping others to do the same."[24] When you teach your TCKs to work through their emotions during their developmental years, they will develop into highly emotionally intelligent adults who can recognize, process, and express their emotions well.

THE MAIN IDEAS:

- Begin using a broad vocabulary of feeling words. Consider printing an emotions chart to aid with this.
- Narrate your young children's emotions, and ask about your older children's feelings.
- Give your children permission to experience and express all emotions, and guide them in doing so in an appropriate way.
- Begin daily family check-ins.
- Remember that teaching your TCKs to experience, express, and process their emotions will help them grow into emotionally intelligent adults.

QUESTIONS TO CONSIDER:

- How can you begin using feeling words in your family? Where are some good places to keep your feelings charts?
- How will it feel for your family to begin talking about feelings more? Are their certain family members who will be more uncomfortable than others?
- How do you think your family will respond to the idea of family check-ins? When can you begin implementing them?

CHAPTER 3

Tuning In to your TCK's Needs

Healthy TCKs are in-tune to the emotional needs of others because they have either had their needs met by intentional, engaging, healthy parents during their developmental years, or they have processed and grieved the pain of unmet needs.

Babies communicate their needs with their first cry and continue to do so in different ways as they grow and develop more complex methods of communicating. When these needs are met by loving parents, children feel safe and secure and are likely to thrive developmentally. When these needs aren't met, it is a recipe for behavior problems, relational difficulties, mental health disorders, and many other issues. It can seem like these "needs" are purely physical, but that is only a part of it. The other equally important part is the more ambiguous realm of *emotional* needs. Tuning into your TCKs' needs by creating an emotionally safe environment develops the brain functions needed for them to live healthy adult lives. This area of emotional safety is unfortunately one that I often find is lacking in even the most well-meaning expatriate families. In my work I have found three factors that contribute to this:

1- The tremendous pressure on expatriate families to perform. Most expatriate families feel like they live in a fishbowl because they are more publicly visible due to their unique lives. This almost always puts extra pressure on parents to present the "perfect family" persona. Often, meeting the needs of children means doing things that could be unpopular (not showing up for that event, taking a day off to spend with a child, allowing a child to voice that they don't love the new country they are in, etc.), and thus, if parents succumb to the pressure, the TCK's emotional needs may not be prioritized.

2- Lack of emotional capacity. It is during the most high-stress times that TCKs' need for emotional support goes up while their parents' mental and physical capacities to meet their children's needs (and even their own!) goes down.

This often results in stressed-out parents who have children with unmet emotional needs. Even the most fabulous, attentive parents can run into this challenge if it is not consciously combatted. When entering a new culture, the parents themselves are in survival mode for a while, attempting to find their footing in an entirely new environment. The children are simultaneously relying on these highly stressed parents for assurance of safety, security, and emotional stability as they also attempt to find a new normal. Unfortunately, this combination can often result in the children subconsciously feeling as if their emotional needs are not being met.

3 - Assuming the needs are met. When families have lived overseas long enough for it to feel normal, it can be easy to slip into a rhythm of life that isn't actively attentive to the TCK's needs. Even if TCKs are thriving, parents should not stop tuning in and checking in with their TCKs. Because the challenges of the TCK life are often stacked (happening one after the other) and unresolved grief is such a common issue (more on that in chapter 5), parents of TCKs need to be extra vigilant about being an emotional support to them—even if they don't appear to need it.

Not only is meeting the emotional needs of children critical in the child's own health and development, but if a child's emotional needs go routinely unmet throughout their childhood, it is likely to affect their own parenting one day, thus creating a vicious generational cycle. This is a common issue that we are seeing in adult TCKs as they become parents themselves. By looking at ways to address emotional needs during your child's life spent overseas and particularly during the transition to and from living overseas, you can prevent this cycle from occurring and strengthen your relationship with your TCK.

MEETING YOUR OWN NEEDS

In order to be emotionally available to your children, you have to be first in tune with your own emotional needs. It is similar to the idea of putting on your own oxygen mask first. Everyone who's ever traveled via airplane knows the spiel:

"In the event of a decompression, an oxygen mask will automatically appear in front of you. To start the flow of oxygen, pull the mask toward you. Place it firmly over your nose and mouth, secure the elastic band behind your head, and breathe normally. Although the bag does not inflate, oxygen is flowing to the mask. If you are traveling with a child or someone who requires assistance, secure your mask on first, and then assist the other person."

You know you're a TCK when you can write that from memory as I just did.

This protocol is not only useful for decompressed aircrafts but also an important illustration for parenting children overseas. Parents are often concerned about the well-being of their children, as they should be, but it is equally as important for you to be concerned about your own well-being. If your own oxygen mask is not secured first, then you are not going to be helpful to your child. If your own emotional and physical needs are not well tended, you will not be able to be the parent that your child needs you to be. This is particularly true when you are moving and living overseas.

It can be very easy to sacrifice your own emotions and needs on the altars of productivity and caring for everyone else. It might even seem more selfless, or strong, or godly, or holy to forgo your own needs for the sake of your children, but not only is this not sustainable, it teaches your children to do the same.

Children are the world's best copycats. How you process your own emotions and work through challenging situations directly impacts how your child will do so. This impacts their "little years" and sets the patterns for the rest of their life. If a child who lives overseas watches her mother or father ignore their own needs and emotions, she will be more likely to do the same as a child, teenager, and adult.

In uncomfortable or traumatic situations, like moving overseas or sitting in an oxygen-leaking airplane, you have the opportunity to choose how you are going to respond. As a parent the natural response is to get the oxygen mask on your kid, to make sure they are transitioning well, to tend to their grief as they move to a new country, and to help them wade through the uncharted waters of living in a new culture. However, it is critical that this natural response is consciously and continuously reversed and that you first take stock of your own emotions and needs.

Here is a simple process for this:

- **Pause and listen to your thoughts.**
- **Name your feelings.** Are you frustrated, anxious, nervous, sad, afraid?
- **Ask why.** What is the source of each of these feelings? Can you pinpoint when that exact feeling started? What was the trigger?
- **How is that feeling affecting you?** Are you speaking more sharply to your children? Are you slamming doors? Is your tone of voice different because of your feelings?
- **Respond.** Now that you have taken stock of your current emotions and how they might be affecting you, work through it. Do you need a good cry? Some alone time? A cup of coffee? A nap? Find a way to tend to each emotion in some fashion. Avoid ignoring it, and instead work through it in a healthy way. Perhaps even say to your child, "Mommy is feeling a bit frustrated right now and needs to take some deep breaths and drink a cup of tea. Would you like to do that with me?" This is the process of putting on your own oxygen mask, so to speak, so that you can then tend to your child's needs more effectively and modeling it to your child in the process.

When you, the parent, are going through the transition of moving to a new country or working through the challenges of living overseas, don't hold your breath and push through it for the sake of helping your children. Instead, put on your own oxygen mask first, take a deep breath, and then tend to your children. The chances of long-term emotional thriving are much higher for both the parent and the child when the parent is willing to do the work of tending to his or her own needs.

MEETING THEIR NEED TO FEEL VALUED

I would argue that the most important words that TCKs need to hear from their parents are these: "You are more important than our work."

These words never being spoken causes a deep-seated heart issue for many TCKs that contributes directly to difficulty building healthy relationships, poor—or exceedingly high—performance in school and work, and even mental health disorders. I can give parents a million tools for helping their children adjust to a life overseas and to prevent common TCK issues, but none of that will be effective if a child believes in their core that their parents are more passionate about their work than about loving and parenting them.

I have talked with and read stories and blogs of countless TCKs who felt that they were far less important than the work their parents went overseas to do. Parenting was just a required, inconvenient task.

I would guess that if you asked the parents of these TCKs, they would be astounded that their children felt this way. They would say, "But we put them in the best schools!" "We took them to amazing vacation spots!" "We made sure they were able to bring their special toys with them when we moved!" and so on. While these actions can contribute to a child's feeling of being loved, they do not replace the need for the craved words, "You are more important than our work."

Because of the nature of overseas work, it is easy for children to perceive that the people their parents moved overseas to minister to, or the company they went to work for, or the country whose military they serve are clearly their first priority. After all, those entities and people groups literally dictate everything about their lives—even where they live! Though it may not be the truth, children can quickly feel that they are second place to the job that moved their family across the globe. Sadly, this belief can accompany them through life and into adulthood.

It can be especially easy for overseas workers, whose personal lives and work are so interwoven, to let parenting take the back burner. Show your TCKs that they are so valuable and cherished and loved and that being their parent *is* your most important job. Then tell them, "You are more important than our work," over and over and over.

MEETING THEIR NEEDS BY ENGAGING

It is important for parents raising children anywhere to be continually engaging and checking in with their kids. This level of relationship provides the emotional support and stability that they desperately need. This emotional presence often begins by simply checking in with children and asking questions. Because TCKs are privy to struggles that monocultural children don't often have to face, the questions you should be asking are also unique to their experience. Engaging with your TCKs in this way is also important because, as we just discussed, your work and your home life are often very intermixed. It can feel to many TCKs that there is not time set aside for them to receive their parents' undivided attention and presence.

Set aside time routinely to talk with your TCKs. Ensure that this time is not tainted by distractions and that you are not attempting to multitask, but instead be fully engaged and interested in their answers. If these types of conversations are not something you have had with your TCKs in the past, it may take some time before they truly trust that you care about their answers and that they are safe to answer honestly. For this reason, it is critical to create a safe space for them to speak openly. Listen and encourage them to explain their answers or elaborate but be careful not to be too pushy or to respond in a way that invalidates their answers. Remember that the purpose of asking these questions is not to provide a solution but to open up the communication between you and your children.

Here are some questions to guide your conversations. You might ask your TCKs all of these questions, or just have them on hand to ask one or two questions when you're spending time with them.

1. **How are you doing?**
    It seems simple, but asking this question is one of the best ways to show your TCK that you care. Make it clear that there isn't a right answer and that it is okay if they really aren't doing "just fine."

2. **What are some things you enjoy about living here?**
    Their "favorites" may be different than you expect!

3. **Do you ever wish that we lived a different life?**

    It's important to help your TCK process the life that they are living. It is unique and it wasn't of their choosing. It's healthy for them to think through this question and for you to hear their answers as they may reveal some deeper struggles that need to be worked through.

4. **What is something that you're looking forward to?**

    This gives your TCK the opportunity to share their excitement about an upcoming event. Perhaps you didn't know about this event or didn't realize how important it is to your child. Now that you know, you can share in their excitement!

5. **What is something that you're not looking forward to?**

    This question often provides the opportunity to dig deeper and discover why a certain event, place, task, etc. is unenjoyable or uncomfortable for your child. Avoid a positive comeback such as, "But that will be so fun!" and instead explore the question further by saying something like, "Wow, I didn't realize that place made you nervous. What is it about it that is uncomfortable to you?"

6. **Do you feel like we spend enough time together?**

    Like we discussed, TCKs can often feel like they are second to their parents' work or ministry. This question allows your child the opportunity to say so if that is the case. If their answer is no, be vigilant about finding ways to spend more time with this child.

7. **Where do you feel most at home?**

   The question "Where is home?" is a common, confusing question for TCKs. Working through this idea at a young age prevents it from becoming a surprising realization when they are older and feel that no place feels completely like "home."

8. **Is there anyone or anything that you miss right now?**

   It is important to give TCKs the permission to reminisce and grieve their losses. Bringing these up for them can help them to do this in a healthy way.

9. **Do you feel like people understand you?**

   Being a TCK can create the feeling of being misunderstood. Hearing your TCK's answer to this question can be helpful as you help them to learn to anchor their identity, which we'll talk about in chapter 7.

10. **What is your favorite thing about yourself?**

    Because identity issues are common for TCKs, asking them to think through things that they like about themselves is a good way to promote self-confidence. This is also a good time to tell them a few of *your* favorite things about them!

MEETING THEIR NEEDS THROUGH INTENTIONALITY

You know your children and can sense when they are "off," but sometimes the stress of moving can cause parents to forget to pay attention to their children's emotions. Be sensitive and mindful about what they may be feeling and be willing to take the necessary actions to respond well to those feelings.

Pay attention to their personality and temperament and use this insight to determine how you can act upon it. Are they introverted? Extroverted? Independent? Anxiety prone? How might these things play into their emotions during a move? Has your introvert had too much people time? Does your independent child feel like he's expected to be strong and independent so that he doesn't burden you? Does your anxious child feel stressed about the upcoming plane ride? Only by knowing your children can you really identify what their emotional needs are and take the correct actions.

Be intentional about finding ways for them to recharge. Young children are not in tune with their emotions enough to know what they need in order to feel refreshed, and older children may need to be coached through self-care. Figure out what your children need to recharge themselves, and then help them to do that. This is particularly important during transitions. Does your introvert need some alone time? Is your other child recharged by quality time with you? Does another need some extra snuggles? Time exploring the outdoors? Do you all need a restful pajama day?

It can be easy when you are under stress to hear what your children say but not realize the underlying meaning to their words. Often, emotional needs are communicated very indirectly and yet require attention and action. So when your child says, "Will you play with me?," perhaps what they really mean is, "I need quality time with you." Or when your other, introverted child has an outburst because they don't want to go to another event in the new place, maybe they are saying, "I've met so many new people, and that makes me so tired! I just need some alone time to recharge!" Listen for the needs and be the advocate for getting their needs met.

It takes extra time and energy to tune in and be sensitive to your children's needs, especially when you yourself are struggling to find your footing in the midst of transition and living cross-culturally. But it is so important that you are meeting their emotional needs. Not only does it help to foster your relationships with your children, but it sets them up to be people who can identify their own needs and eventually the needs of their own children.

RELATED BENEFITS — AN EMOTIONALLY HEALTHY LEGACY:

The benefits that come to children whose parents were intentional about meeting their emotional needs are endless. The ACE scores and toxic stress that we discussed can be completely prevented when children's needs are met and thus, they are likely to be healthy adults, healthy parents one day, and raise healthy kids of their own. By fostering emotional health in your TCK, you are equipping them with an invaluable gift that will allow for and enhance health in all other areas of the TCK life.

THE MAIN IDEAS:

- You cannot adequately meet your children's needs without first meeting your own.

- TCKs are privy to feeling subpar to their parents' work. Verbalize that they are cherished, valued, and more important than your work.
- Engage with your TCKs by checking in regularly and asking questions that lead to deeper conversations.
- Be intentional about recognizing the unique needs of each of your children and seeking to meet those needs in a healthy way.

QUESTIONS TO CONSIDER:

- What are the personalities and temperaments of each of your children?
- What exhausts them and what recharges them?
- In what areas have you been effectively meeting their emotional needs?
- What are some ways you could grow and be more intentional about meeting your TCKs' emotional needs?

CHAPTER 4

Learning How to Leave Well

Healthy TCKs allow themselves to love people and places enough to feel the pain of each loss and give themselves permission to grieve each time they leave or are left.

I fell asleep in the car as we left my aunt's house in San Jose, California, to head home to Modesto, about a two-hour drive. To my surprise and horror, I woke up in a motel room and had no recollection of moving from the car to the bed that I woke up in. Much to my relief, I found my parents in the adjacent room and soon found out that they had taken a surprise detour to Santa Cruz where we would spend the rest of the weekend playing at the beach and exploring the famous boardwalk. I was convinced that I had the coolest parents ever. Sometime during our stay there, my parents sat my brother and me down on the motel bed and told us that we would be moving to Africa in six months. Once I realized they weren't joking, the news sank in and I went through a kaleidoscope of emotions. Excited, nervous, happy, anxious, thrilled, scared. But mostly excited. For about three months. As the reality and gravity of the move set in, I slid from mostly excited to mostly scared, nervous, sad, upset, and angry. The closer we got to moving day, the more terrible the idea sounded. As we went from church to church support-raising, I struggled to keep a smile on my face through the grief that was brewing under the surface. Sometimes I was good at playing the part of the happy missionary kid, but most of the time, I was not. Especially the closer we got to our moving date.

Whether the first move or tenth, leaving never ceases to be one of the most difficult aspects of the TCK life. So many feelings—either new or all too familiar—arise with the sinking anticipation of the transition ahead. This season is often the first critical "touch point" in which TCKs need proactive preventive care. They are raw, unaware—or all too aware—of what is to come. The impending difficulties, while it will ache to watch them slog through them, can ultimately weave together brilliant resilience, empathy, perspective, and so many other incredible qualities if fostered carefully. If you have already "left," you know the ache I speak of, and I pray that the tools I offer in this chapter will give you more strategies for navigating future moves. If you have not yet launched into your first big transition, I truly desire that this brings about hope and confidence, knowing that while we can never diminish the difficulty of leaving, we can teach ourselves and our TCKs how to navigate it proactively.

I have learned from my own experience of moving overseas, and now watching hundreds of families move overseas, that there is a natural progression that children (and adults) go through as they lead up to the big move. The closer they get to moving day, the more they struggle with leaving. What was exciting about the move six months prior is now a daunting, grief-inducing reality in the days and weeks before leaving day.

I have heard it said that tension is good, and I believe that this is especially true in regard to TCKs. As hard as that tension is, it is an essential part of leaving well and grieving well, and it is important that you allow your children and yourself to experience that tension fully.

Teaching your children at a young age to "put on a happy face" creates a breeding ground for unresolved grief and attachment issues later in their life. When you teach your children to ignore the tension, you are teaching them not to care.

A significant issue that has arisen among young adult and adult TCKs is the ability to move from one place to the next, one relationship to the next, one job to the next, without any tension. Without caring. They have learned to ignore the grief, or worse, not to grieve at all because they never cared about the people, job, or place enough to grieve the loss. You can imagine the destruction and devastation this can bring to relationships, careers, families, etc. This combined with the TCK's tendency not to settle and adapt, but instead remain in a surface-level, adapting state, is a lethal combination for TCKs in adulthood.

Your young TCKs will either learn or not learn how to embrace the tension, feel the heartache, and grieve the losses. While it is horribly difficult to watch your children grieve and struggle, remember that the tension means that they care, and you absolutely do not want to raise TCKs who stop caring.

This is a clear picture of the ampersand nature of TCK life—this tension between wanting to protect our children from feeling difficult feelings and also realizing that it is an important part of their ability to reap the benefits of the TCK life. If we don't embrace this tension, we will constantly be trying to protect them to no avail from the very things that could ultimately breed so many amazing attributes. It is only through extreme temperature and pressure that diamonds are made, and likewise healthy TCKs. When we try to shield TCKs from the challenges of this unique lifestyle, not only will we be unsuccessful, but we will also be keeping them from the richness of their Third Culture Kid upbringing.

RAFT

Throughout the remainder of this book, I will mention the acronym RAFT with various applications. The original version comes from David Pollock and Ruth Van Reken in their book *Third Culture Kids 3rd Edition: Growing Up Among Worlds*.[25] I will give a short description of the acronym below for you to refer to. The acronym was developed as a guide for leaving well.

R = Reconciliation. In other words, say sorry. Make amends with anyone whom you may have hurt or been hurt by before moving. TCKs quickly learn that they can forgo the discomfort of having hard conversations with friends by simply getting on an airplane. This far too easily becomes a habit. Teach them from a young age that reconciling before a move is not optional, and model that for them by reconciling where you need to as well.

A = Affirmation. Tell the people you love that you love them. Help your TCKs write thank-you cards or draw pictures for their friends and family. Perhaps make a list together as a family of all the people to whom you want to say "Thank you" or "I love you" before you leave, and then include your children when you do so.

F = Farewell. Say good-bye, not only to people, but to places and things as well. This is especially important for young children.

Take a final trip to their favorite park, schedule final playdates, say good-bye. It is critical to the grieving process that children know it is the *final* playdate, trip to the park, night sleeping in their bed, etc. and are able to say good-bye. A fun idea is to give your child a disposable camera to take pictures of all of these "lasts." Then print them and put them in a photo album for your child to keep.

T = Think Destination. Talk with your kids about the place where you will be moving. What do you know about it? What might be different from where you are living now? What is the plan when you first arrive? Perhaps watch YouTube videos, look at pictures of where you will be living, or plan to do something fun when you first arrive. This gives your family something fun to look forward to immediately!

It is important during this stage to be careful not to compare. It can be easy to say things that suggest that "there" will be *better than* "here." This not only can lead to discouragement but can contribute to an issue of subconscious expectations that we'll address in chapter 12.

PACKING

The packing process is often the first time that the idea of leaving "home" and moving to a new country or city becomes a tangible reality for children. As parents you have been planning for months and have likely had many "reality checks," but your children may have not had the same experiences. Packing up their bedrooms makes the reality of what is about to happen significantly more concrete. During this process, and a repeat of it during any subsequent moves, you may find that your children are suddenly incredibly sentimental and the toys they haven't played with in years, stuffed animals they haven't touched since birth, and craft supplies they haven't been interested in for months become their most prized possessions that they can't possibly move to another country without. This can be frustrating for you, as you are trying strategically to pack six fifty-pound bags filled with everything you need to start a life in a new country. It can be equally as frustrating for your child who is suddenly realizing that life is about to change drastically, and the toys, animals, and craft supplies in his or her room seem to be the only things that he or she might be able to hold onto.

As I packed my room at thirteen years old to move to Africa, everything became sentimental. I distinctly remember sitting on my bedroom floor in California, crying about having to throw away a tardy slip that I had been given for being late to my sixth-grade science class. I begged my parents to let me keep it. I wouldn't have been able to explain it then but having to throw away that pink tardy slip was a physical representation of leaving that life, that school, to start over in a new place worlds away. It wasn't "just trash." My gracious parents realized this and held me as I cried, letting the reality sink in that I would never again receive another pink tardy slip from my junior high school.

During a trip back to the US my sophomore year in high school, we went shopping at IKEA. As we were leaving, my mom spotted a string of battery-operated lights shaped like stars and walked back in and bought them for me. This sort of thing was pretty atypical for her, so it has always been a favorite memory of mine. Those star lights hung in my room in California, my room in two different cities in Tanzania, my college dorm room, and my first apartment. That silly string of lights signified "home" for me for years and created a sense of comfort during many moves and many hard nights all over the globe. They officially died after I married my husband and I simultaneously didn't feel the need for them any longer.

As you're packing your children's things, remember that it's not "just stuff." While they may not be able to take everything with them that they would like to, take the time to let them grieve over what they are losing. The tears may not actually be about the tardy slip or the pillowcase; those are just tangible reminders of the bigger, deeper losses that are on the horizon. Let them keep something or help them find or create something new, like star lights or a stuffed animal, that signifies "home" for them. While packing can be something that your productive self just wants to "get done," it is a significant part of the grieving process for most children, and patience and understanding on your part can make a huge difference in how well that process is played out.

TEENAGERS

While everything in this book applies in some way to TCKs of all ages, moving overseas with teenagers has some special variables that are important to consider. Having personally moved overseas as a young teen, I can speak to the challenges of uprooting and re-rooting during that season of life. One of the most significant factors to making that transition as healthy and smooth as possible is being intentional about leaving well. Unlike small children, teens will vividly remember the leaving process, and for this reason, leaving in a healthy way is critical for them to grow into healthy adult TCKs.

Here are some things to consider:

Say good-bye well. Help your teenagers to say good-bye well using the RAFT acronym. I have noticed that this doesn't often happen with teenagers because they assume that they will return to their passport countries before long. It is important to keep in mind that while your teenager may only live overseas with you for a short time, in that short time a lot is happening both for them and their peers back home. They will not return to the way life was, and that is a significant loss. Their friends will likely be starting at different colleges in different places, they will likely not be returning to live in the home that they left, they will be returning as an adult, and their peers will also have recently launched into adulthood. They are leaving during one of the most change-filled seasons of life, so while it may be a short time period, it is an incredibly significant time period. Saying good-bye well to their current lives will help them to start a healthy life when they return as an adult.

Make it a family conversation. If possible, talk with your teen-agers about the decision to move overseas, and ask for and listen to their input. While you, the parents, will make the final decision, it is important to let your teenagers know that you respect their opinions on this significant, life-changing decision.

Don't blame hormones. While it can be easy to think of teenage hormones as the culprit for their moodiness or extra-emotional state, remember that while hormones may accentuate the grief of leaving, they do not make that grief any less real. Teenagers are experiencing an extreme loss when they move overseas and often aren't simply "acting like a teenager" when that grief comes out in seemingly exaggerated ways.

Take them seriously. Along with not blaming hormones, it is important to take your teens seriously when they express points of grief or concern to you. While missing the high school dance might not seem like a big deal to you, it very well may be for your teen. Be careful not to downplay their sources of grief or, worse, make fun of them for it.

Provide options for good-byes. I worked with a teenage girl who was about to move to Asia. She wanted to do something special to say good-bye to her best friend, and after talking through some options, she decided that she wanted to make her a scrapbook. We printed pictures of the two of them, shopped for scrapbook paper and stickers, and she made a beautiful keepsake for her friend. Other teens might want to have a pizza night with their close friends before they leave, go to the movies with a group of friends, have a sleepover, etc. Encourage them to think of a way to say good-bye to their friends and help them to make it happen.

Teens are not only moving overseas and becoming TCKs, but they are doing so at a complex time in life. The success of their transition has a direct effect on their wellbeing when they are no longer living under your roof. By being intentional about helping them leave well, you will strengthen your relationships with your teens and ease the transition overseas for your entire family.

GRANDPARENTS

One hot topic that comes up when I work with parents is the struggle of leaving their children's grandparents behind. Moving overseas requires significant sacrifice, and leaving grandparents is a notably hard one. Not only is it hard on you, but the grandparents you leave behind are required to make this sacrifice by no choice of their own.

For some grandparents, they express the sadness of this by resenting the fact that you are taking their grandchildren away from them to some far-off place and depriving them of being actively involved in their grandchildren's lives.

Often this struggle and the tension it creates are not addressed and remains as the elephant in the room, so to speak. It bubbles up in insensitive comments or unspoken bitterness. This is why you need to have "the talk," preferably *before* you move overseas. Here is what I suggest "the talk" should consist of:

- Acknowledge how difficult it is for them to have you leave with their grandchildren. Express that it is incredibly difficult for you as well. Talk about the specific events you are sad that they will miss.

- Talk about why you feel it is important for your family to make this move.

- Share how important it is to you for them to give their blessing, to be supportive of your decision, and to remain involved in your children's lives. Unfortunately, some will not give their blessing. At this point, you have done what you can on your end and you can only pray that they will eventually be able to see why you are making the decision that you are.

- Talk about ways that they can stay actively involved in their grandchildren's lives. With technology today, there are many ways your children's grandparents can remain a significant part of their lives.

Here are some ideas:

Share a meal together regularly. Perhaps begin a Saturday tradition of "breakfast with Grandma and Grandpa." Skype them in and share a meal together. Talk about the week. Depending on the time difference, it may be dinner at Grandma's house and breakfast at yours, but that is okay! Maybe they can eat breakfast for dinner that night.

Share pictures. Have the grandparents ask the children for pictures of their new home, friends, school, etc. This is valuable for a multitude of reasons. The grandparents can be "in the know" when the children talk about a certain place or person, the children are excited that the grandparents *want* to know about their lives, it gives the grandparents questions to ask and conversation topics, and it gives the grandparents a little window into their grandchildren's new world.

Have twin stuffed animals. The grandparents can buy matching stuffed animals, one to give to the children and the other to keep. They can tell the children that when they hug their stuffed animals, they are getting a big hug from Grandma and Grandpa. For older children, they can take pictures of their stuffed animals in different places or during different events and share the pictures back and forth with their grandparents.

Storytime. Grandparents can read the children a story and show them the pictures in the book via WhatsApp or another instant video service. Consider doing this on regular nights so that it becomes part of your routine. When special time with grandparents like this becomes a regular and expected part of the child's life, it encourages intimacy more so than less frequent, more monumental events.

Visit. Perhaps the very best way for grandparents to be a significant part of their grandchildren's lives is to visit them while they are overseas. Their grandchildren have begun a new life in a new culture, and it will be very difficult for them to connect with their grandparents if they have not experienced their lives firsthand. By visiting, grandparents communicate that they want to see and experience the children's new world.

Read about TCKs. I cannot express how strongly I feel about grandparents, and other family members and friends who are significant in the children's lives, reading this book as well as the book *Third Culture Kids 3rd Edition: Growing Up Among Worlds.* It is often hard for family and friends to understand how much your children have changed because of their experience living overseas, especially if you move when they are a bit older. However, from the moment they began their new life overseas, they became a Third Culture Kid (TCK) and have changed in ways that even they probably don't realize. These resources will open grandparents' eyes to how their grandchildren may have changed during their time living overseas.

Making the decision to move overseas doesn't mean that grandparents can't be involved in and play a significant role in their grandchildren's lives. With some effort on your part as parents and on their part as long-distance grandparents, those relationships can grow despite living worlds apart and can even be deeper because of the intentionality they require.

WAITING

Sometimes leaving doesn't happen on schedule. For many globally mobile families, this scenario is all too familiar: plans for relocation are made, the family mentally and physically prepares for a major life change, and then things don't go according to plan, and life is perpetually on hold.

This season of waiting can be one of the most challenging for expat families and especially for the children. If you're in this season, here are some things to consider:

Create routine. Child psychologist Danielle Kaufman says, "Building routines with your children helps them feel safe and provides them with clear boundaries, expectations, and consistency."[26] This is particularly important when life seems to be out of everyone's control. The kids know that things are not going according to plan, and they don't know what that means for them. It is important that they have a certain routine that they know they can expect no matter how unpredictable life is or where in the world they are. This routine is equally as important when you finally move and begin to settle into the new place. Keep in mind that the goal is stability, not rigidity. For this reason, keep the routines general so that they can be replicated anywhere. For example, going to play outside each morning instead of going to the park each morning or having a special breakfast instead of having a pancake breakfast.

Routines could be:

- waking up at the same time each day
- eating breakfast together
- taking baths every other night
- going to play outside each morning
- having an hour of quiet time each afternoon
- eating a special breakfast every Saturday morning
- having nightly family check-ins

By creating a simple and flexible routine, it can be implemented no matter where in the world you are and thus can create a sense of security and consistency for your children during an inconsistent season of life.

Don't be afraid to sign up. After living in Africa for two years as a young teen, I returned with my family to the United States for what we thought was going to be only the summer months. When returning didn't go as planned, we waited, thinking each month that we would be moving back to Africa the next. For a year this meant moving from place to place (eighteen houses total) and not getting involved in the community or signing up for any activities because we "knew" we would be leaving next month. After that year, we realized that we couldn't keep living in transit and I was finally allowed to sign up for a dance team. Though we were still tentatively going back to Africa, and did a year later, it was so healthy for me to spend that year building community, dancing, and having a routine.

If you are in a waiting period and don't know how long it will last, let your kids get involved in sports, dance, theater, whatever activities they are interested in. If you end up having to pull them out to move, that is okay. It is better that they are able to do it for a time than not at all. And if your waiting period grows, like it did for me, from one month to two years, you'll be glad you let your kids participate in something.

Have fun. Fun is the antidote for stress. The waiting period is no doubt a stressful time and is typically also a time when having fun is not the first thing on your mind. Your kids can feel the stress, tension, and anxiety, and few things relieve it like having fun. During this challenging time, make it a point to have fun with your kids. Play on the floor with them, go outside and run around, go to a theme park, or take a road trip. Bring play, humor, and fun into your waiting period. Stressing won't decrease the wait, and having fun can certainly make it better for everyone.

A family came to our training after three years of waiting to move overseas. The wait was long and hard. When they finally made it to their destination overseas, they realized how essential that waiting period was in their preparation for living overseas. As they said, "We were not ready to live overseas. It was the years of waiting that truly prepared us, and we are living healthier lives overseas because of it."

The waiting season is so hard, and I ache for the many families I know who have waited and waited and faced disappointment after disappointment. It can seem, or genuinely be, an endless season of waiting. But during this season, I have seen and experienced the benefits for children of creating routine, signing up for activities, and having fun as a family, and have seen how practicing these things during the wait can set them up for a healthier life once they finally get overseas.

RELATED BENEFITS — HOPE IN ADVERSITY:

"Children with high levels of hopefulness have experience with adversity. They have been given the opportunity to struggle and in doing that they have learned how to believe in themselves."[27] By fostering a healthy leaving process and having the conversations outlined in this chapter, you are preparing your TCKs to be more self-aware individuals who have a toolbox to deal with difficult things, like leaving. This skill is one that is rarely shared by mono-cultural individuals who have not experienced frequent good-byes. While for them a move might be an incredibly stressful event, for TCKs with this skill, it is difficult but not as intense. They develop a beautiful resilience that instills the belief that says, "Even though this hurts and is so hard, I know I will be okay." Because life is messy and rocky, having this refrain etched in their minds from a young age will help them to be strong in the face of challenges throughout their lives.

THE MAIN IDEAS:

- Leave each place well by following the RAFT acronym (Reconciliation, Affirmation, Farewell, and Think Destination).
- Moving with teenagers has unique challenges that need to be addressed differently than those of other age groups.
- Find ways to involve long-distance grandparents as much as possible and to communicate your love and appreciation for them and foster relationship.
- During a waiting period, create as much routine for your children as possible, allow them to engage in activities, and have fun!

QUESTIONS TO CONSIDER:

- How can you begin to implement the RAFT process?
- What steps need to be taken to foster a healthy grandparent relationship while you are overseas?
- What stood out to you as important steps that you need to take as you leave? Or, if you are already living overseas, what might you modify for the next move?

CHAPTER 5

Resolving Unresolved Grief

Healthy TCKs feel, process, and resolve their grief and through it develop a beautiful ability for empathy, connection, and compassion.

If you have spent any time reading about Third Culture Kids, you have almost certainly come across the topics of grief and loss. There is a considerable amount of great content that explains the sources of TCK grief, why the losses are so significant, and why unresolved grief is a common and serious issue. Once again, I highly recommend the book *Third Culture Kids 3rd Edition: Growing Up Among Worlds* to learn more about TCK grief and loss. Taking a preventive care approach, I hope to turn this into a very practical conversation. Beginning with the foundation that grief and loss are unavoidable issues for TCKs, we can then move toward finding ways to prevent these issues from becoming debilitating to TCKs.

Before getting into the prevention of grief-related issues, let's first look at some of the key sources of TCK grief.

FREQUENT GOOD-BYES

My dear friend and her husband have recently become global workers and are heading overseas next year with their eighteen-month-old boy in tow. This past summer they attended a training where they spent two weeks learning with other families. They developed close friendships in this short time.

As they left their training, my friend called and said, "It was so hard to leave people that we just spent two weeks befriending, knowing that we might not ever see them again. And then I realized, this is the life that we're signing up for. And not just us—this is the life we are signing our son up for as well."

Around the same time, I finished up a summer culture and language training for families. One of the little girls in my class, a four-year-old, was having a difficult time during the first couple of days and didn't want to make friends. She had moved overseas and back to the United States before, and though she was only four, she knew what it felt like to make friends and then have to leave them. I think that she sensed this coming. But sure enough, by the end of the week she had overcome her apprehension and become best buddies with the other girls in the class.

As she finally began to make friends, I felt the tension along with her. I was silently cheering her on but also dreading the good-byes I knew she would have to say in a few days.

Her subconscious fears that kept her from making friends were not incorrect. In fact, they were incredibly accurate.

TCKs are assigned to a life of frequent good-byes. Even if they do not move often themselves, the expatriate community in general tends to be a very transient one. This creates a revolving-door atmosphere that results in people constantly going in and out of TCKs' lives.

When good-byes are so frequent, it can be easy simply to decide to stop trying to build relationships. It is not uncommon for TCKs to think, "Why would I? It's not worth it. I know it won't last and

I'll have to say good-bye and I know how much that hurts."

It can be easy to want to reassure them, to encourage them to keep investing in friendships, or to set up playdates so they can make a new set of friends. I am not discouraging this, but I do want us to consider the downside of what we are proposing with this attitude. To the TCKs who have said frequent good-byes, it may sound like, "It's not that bad. This is just our life. You'll get over the loss. You'll make new friends in no time. You'll be fine."

So, while you should absolutely encourage your TCKs to connect and make friends, it is equally important to acknowledge how hard it is to leave friends and the grief that comes with it. Though difficult, TCKs need to experience the sadness of the losses. They need to sit in the grief and allow themselves to process. If they don't, then they may adopt the attitude, "It's not that bad. This is just my life. I'll get over the loss in no time. I'll make new friends in no time. I'll be fine." This mentality is not uncommon for TCKs, and the consequence is a growing lack of attachment. In each new place they may make new friends, but they never allow themselves to invest emotionally in those people and friendships enough to be sad about leaving them when the time comes. They stop caring enough to grieve the loss.

HIDDEN LOSSES

Much of the TCK's grief stems from losses that are neither obvious nor acknowledged. These hidden losses often remain buried in the underground parts of the TCK's psyche, creating a toxic soil that can result in unresolved grief. Unfortunately, the sprouts of these seeds of hidden losses inevitably spring up to the surface sooner or later in destructive and unhealthy patterns. This most commonly happens when a TCK reaches adulthood.

How can you uncover these "hidden losses" so that they can be called out, acknowledged, and productively and preventively worked through? First, we need to recognize what these hidden losses commonly are. The following list comes from *Third Culture Kids 3rd Edition* by David Pollock, Ruth Van Reken, and Michael Pollock.[28]

Loss of their world. TCKs lose everything they know, all at once, with an airplane ride. This often happens repeatedly and sometimes without warning.

Loss of status. Not only do TCKs lose their world, but they lose their sense of place in it. They no longer know where they fit and what they have to offer as a person in each new culture.

Loss of lifestyle. The daily routines, housing type, and way of life often change nearly instantaneously with each move.

Loss of possessions. This doesn't only include favorite toys that are left behind, but it also means things that connect TCKs to their past. These could be dishes, their bedding, the Christmas tablecloth that signaled the holiday season, Dad's favorite rocking chair, etc.

Loss of relationships. Whether they are the ones leaving or being left, TCKs often lose friends routinely. They are also more likely to have disrupted relationships within their nuclear families (siblings at boarding school, parents traveling for work or ministry, grandparents a continent away, etc.).

Loss of a past that wasn't. Birthday parties missed, not graduating with the high school class they started with, not being close with friends and family in the passport country. This loss encompasses all the things they would have been a part of if they hadn't moved away.

Loss of the past that was. Being unable to go back to the past as they remember it. Because people may have moved on or the physical places they remember may no longer be accessible, there is no tangible way to remember the life that happened in a certain place.

"The real issue is that in these types of invisible losses, where the tangible and intangible are so inextricably intertwined, no one actually died or was divorced, and nothing was physically stolen. They were all surrounded with so much good."[29]

Hidden losses often remain hidden in the TCK's life because they go unacknowledged by the parents either purposefully to avoid talking about the "sad stuff" or unintentionally because they may not be as obvious or impactful to the parent.

By simply being aware, you can prevent unresolved grief from accompanying these hidden losses. Perhaps you have never thought about these losses being so grief-inducing for your TCKs, or maybe you just never connected words and specific losses to the struggles you have seen in your TCKs. Awareness does not take away the losses, but it does give you a clearer window into what your child might be going through, and by being intentional about bringing them out of hiding, you prevent the unresolved grief issue that is the result of letting these losses remain hidden.

WHY IS GRIEVING IMPORTANT?

Each of the losses that TCKs experience are like toy blocks that stack on top of one another. I call this the Grief Tower. With each loss or grief-inducing experience, another block is stacked on the tower. When TCKs don't grieve those losses, the blocks remain on the tower and continue to be stacked up and up. Eventually, the tower will topple over and the TCK will have to deal with the grief in some way. Some do this by numbing emotion. When the tower topples over, they consciously or subconsciously choose to stop paying any attention to the tower. While it may look harmless from the outside, numbing is not a healthy way of dealing with grief.

In *Dare to Lead*, Brené Brown tells us, "We cannot successfully numb emotion. If we numb the dark, we numb the light. If we take the edge off pain and discomfort, we are, by default, taking the edge off joy, love, belonging, and other emotions that give meaning to our lives."[30]

Numbing emotion is a skill I mastered as a young TCK during my years of transition, loss, and traumatic events. I became excellent at not caring, at being strong and independent, and was seemingly unphased by events that would be grief-inducing for most. The great thing, I thought, about this approach to not grieving is that it looked very successful. I looked like I was doing quite well despite all that I had gone through. I was not an angry child or teen, I was not turning to substances or unhealthy behaviors, I seemed to be a parent's dream child—holding it all together through the difficult times, easily adaptable, excelling in school, well behaved, etc. I felt like I had successfully usurped the challenging TCK life. Fifteen years, marriage, and two kids later, I realized that my skillful ability to power-off my emotions, push through, and put on a great facade so that no one would know my lack of feeling, was a very unhealthy performance that I could not keep up.

This is a common trend for TCKs, especially those who

- feel the need to be/look successful,
- feel they don't have permission/opportunity to grieve,
- feel they will let people down if they are not strong,
- have a deep need and desire to be independent and have it all together,
- have parents who do not demonstrate a healthy grieving process.

Some, like myself, struggle with this only internally and are able to keep it hidden and contained—for a while. Others may turn to addictive substances and other unhealthy behaviors when their grief tower collapses.

One adult TCK said to me, "I couldn't handle the intensity of my emotions any other way than by sleeping with any guy that would take me. My emotions were just too intense for me to deal with, and I had no other release."

Like for that TCK, the emotions, no matter how well TCKs stuff them, have to eventually come out at some point in some way. The Grief Tower can only grow so tall before it comes crashing down.

Let's look at the different elements of grieving and how we can guide TCKs in unstacking their Grief Tower.

PRE-GRIEVING VERSUS POST-GRIEVING

During the moving period, it is important to recognize that there is a continuum of grief that everyone falls on. Tanya Crossman writes about this in *Misunderstood: The Impact of Growing Up Overseas in the 21st Century*: "Some people grieve in advance of a loss—they see it coming and feel sad. They look around and realise, 'I will never do this again.' Others grieve after the change occurs. It is at this point the post-griever realises, 'I will never do this again.'"[31]

People fall on all different points of the continuum between pre-grieving and post-grieving, but I have seen in my work that children in particular tend to lean fairly heavily toward one end or the other. I have found that adding this concept into the toolbox of parents gives them a relieving insight into why their children are responding the way they are. They are then able to be a better support to each child as they do the heaviest part of their grieving.

Children who are pre-grievers will experience the bulk of grief *before* they move overseas. They will grieve the losses that they know are coming even if they can't completely comprehend what those losses will be. Other children are post-grievers. While they still may be sad just before the big move, they will wait until they have arrived in the new place before they fully experience the grief of their losses. Either form of grief is subconscious and is largely determined by the personalities of your children. If you are aware that each of your children will likely fall into one of these categories, then you can be all the more strategic about how you help each child process his or her grief.

PRE-GRIEVING

Below are signs that your child may be a pre-griever and tips for walking with your pre-grieving child through the leaving and grieving process. If you are already living overseas, think back on your child's temperament during you last transition and see if these points apply to them.

Pulling away early. The pre-grieving child will typically experience the bulk of their grief during the three months leading up to the move, and it will usually get progressively worse the closer it gets to moving day. During this time, they may begin to distance themselves from the people, places, things they know they are going to be leaving. They may express disinterest in spending time with friends, going to favorite places, even playing with favorite toys. They know that they will be leaving them soon, so to avoid the pain of the loss, they will "leave" on their own terms in order to feel a sense of control over the leaving. If you notice your child doing this, you need to be especially intentional about helping them through the process of leaving well, as we discussed in chapter 4.

Unusual fears and anxiety. Children who are pre-grievers may express unusual fears and/or experience anxiety. They may talk about these things, but more likely you will notice it through their behavior (not wanting to ride in the car, a sudden fear of being alone, etc.). If you notice these things in your child, address them and talk about them. Simply talking through them out loud may ease their fears.

Poor performance in school. A common theme in children moving overseas is poor performance in school in the months leading up to the move. For pre-grievers, this is an especially likely scenario. In the midst of their grief they are often unable to concentrate well. As they begin to distance themselves and pull away early, this may include school as well. They think, "Why strive to do well if I'm leaving anyway?" The signs for this are obvious: poor grades, unsatisfactory reports from teachers, refusal to do homework, etc. If you notice this becoming an issue for any of your children, address it with them and remind them of your expectations, but be sure you also acknowledge the underlying cause: grief. It may also be helpful to have a conversation with their teachers so that they understand what may be influencing performance in school.

Bad behavior. Young children don't understand the complex emotion of grief, and they don't know how to channel the uncomfortable feelings they are experiencing. This often results in anger about the situation, and this usually manifests in bad behavior. I have heard from many parents, "My child has always been such a well-behaved, respectful kid, but all of a sudden he is acting out! I don't know what's gotten into him!" I answer, "Grief. Grief has gotten into him." While grief may explain the poor behavior, grief does not justify poor behavior. However, the way that you deal with the poor behavior may be different from the way you would parent under "normal" circumstances. Instead of automatically disciplining your child for their bubbling anger, use the opportunity to teach them how to diffuse it in a healthy way.

CARING FOR YOUR PRE-GRIEVER

If you've identified one of your TCKs as a pre-griever, here are some practical ways to care for them as they grieve.

Name the grief. Explain to your child the feeling of grief and how it sometimes bubbles out as anger.

Provide a solution. Explain that while it is okay to be angry and that it is a normal response to the yucky feelings of grief, there are good ways and bad ways to express that anger. The "Get Out My Angry Cards" is a tool that I developed and teach kids ages three all the way to eighteen. I'll admit, I have mentally drawn from my own deck of "Get Out My Angry Cards" a time or two myself! These cards give kids choices for appropriate ways to deal with their anger and other negative emotions. As I stress to the TCKs in my trainings, "It is okay to be angry, but it is not okay to hurt people or yourself in your anger, *and* you must find a way to 'get out your angry' so that it doesn't explode." You'd be surprised how many kids look up at me with big, shocked eyes. But it is true: emotions are never wrong, how you act upon them is a different story. The "Get Out My Angry Cards" tool gives children healthy ways to combat their negative emotions without ignoring them.

Here's how you can make a deck of your own:

Together with your children, brainstorm appropriate ideas for cooling down when they are angry. These could include:

- counting to 100
- journaling
- doing jumping jacks
- listening to music
- going for a walk
- praying about it
- drawing your anger
- taking five deep breaths
- talking about it with someone you trust
- turn on music and dance

Write and/or draw them on three-by-five cards, decorate the cards, hole-punch them, and clip them together with a binder ring. They now have a deck of choices for working through their negative emotions. Every child processes differently, so providing them with a variety of healthy options can be very effective. When you see your child becoming angry, you can instruct him or her to choose a "Get Out My Angry Card" and then proceed to have a conversation about the underlying cause of their anger *after they have completed the card.* Children cannot have a rational conversation in the heat of their anger, so it is critical to wait until their anger has subsided before trying to discuss the subsurface feelings. The cards give them practical ways to cool down, and creating them can be a fun project to do together as a family.

Help them leave well. If you notice your child pulling away early, you will need to be especially intentional about helping them to leave well.

R= Reconciliation. Don't let your pre-grieving child distance themselves from people prematurely. This can lead to broken relationships, especially if they do so quite a while before the move. If this has happened, make sure that your child has the opportunity to reconcile with friends before the move.

A = Affirmation. Help your children write Thank You cards or draw pictures for their friends and family as opposed to pulling away with no good-bye.

F = Farewell. Encourage your child to continue to engage with their friends, favorite places, and favorite things up until it is time to leave. When it is time to leave, take them to say a final farewell.

T = Think Destination. Pre-grievers benefit greatly from having something to look forward to when they arrive in the new place. This eases those final months of intense grief. Consider creating a fun post-arrival plan.

Name the losses. If your child seems to be a pre-griever, it is important that you spend time naming the losses before the move. This will help them to process that grief they are feeling. On a piece of paper, have them write or draw what they will miss when they leave. These should be people, places, and things. As difficult as it is, keep yourself from saying positive things like, "You'll make new friends!" "We'll see Grandma next year!" "I'm sure you'll find a new favorite park!" Instead, allow them to just dwell on the losses. Allow them to cry and to grieve.

Being aware that your child tends to be a pre-griever can be very helpful in knowing the best ways to support them. It will be less of a surprise when they are swallowed by grief in the days and months leading up to the move, and you will be more equipped and willing to comfort and support them, knowing that this is a part of their personal grieving process. The pre-grieving child needs considerable patience, as they are grieving in the midst of the packing, planning, support-raising, good-bye-party chaos. You will have so much on your plate, and taking the time to help your child work through their grief may seem overwhelming, but it is so, so important in order to help them start a healthy life overseas. It can also be helpful to know that they will likely do very well when you arrive overseas. They are doing the very healthy work of grieving before they go, so when you arrive, it is very possible that they will jump right in and embrace life in a new culture.

Be an example. Children need an example of how to deal with complex feelings like grief in a healthy way so let them see you grieve. Talk about how much you will miss people, places, and things. Tell them that you feel yucky inside, too, sometimes when you think about leaving. If you are having a hard time sleeping because of your anxiety about the move, tell them. You may find that they have been having a hard time sleeping too. This will encourage your children to share their grief with you instead of feeling like they have to hide it because they think you won't understand.

I once worked with a family whose five-year-old was having difficulty sleeping. He would lie awake for much of the night, sick to his stomach. I encouraged the father to talk to his son and be open about his own feelings of grief. It turned out, the father was having trouble sleeping as well. One evening he shared with his son that he sometimes can't sleep because he is worried about things regarding the move. The son was so surprised that his father also had trouble sleeping. Through that conversation, his struggle was normalized, he felt closer to his father, and they were able to talk about their struggles with sleep and grief openly.

POST-GRIEVING

The post-grieving child will experience the bulk of their grief after they have arrived overseas when they can "see" what they have lost. The post-grieving child may not seem to be overly upset in the days leading up to the move and instead will enter into the fullness of their grief during the first few days, weeks, even months after you've arrived in the new place.

Post-grieving children often seem comfortable and excited for the pending adventure, so if that sounds like your child, this should signal you that you may have a post-griever on your hands.

Below are things to watch for:

Unemotional good-byes. Post-grievers may not be as emotional as you think they "should" be in the days leading up to the move. This is because they don't feel the weight of the move until after you've landed overseas. They might not feel the need to say good-bye to things or places and may only want to give a quick hug and say "see you later" to their closest friends. This is not because they don't care but because the grief of the good-byes won't fully hit them until they have already left. However, it is vital that you are intentional about walking them through the process of leaving well, part of which is saying good-bye and not "see you later."

Seeming unfazed by the pending move. Post-grievers seem to be the perfect TCKs as you get ready for the big move. They tell everyone how excited they are to move to a new country and can give all sorts of facts about where they will be living. They are sad to pack up their rooms and cut down their stuff to a fifty-pound suitcase, but they are not overly upset about it. If this is your child, be prepared to have a bit of a rough start when you arrive overseas. They may ease right into the new country, but more likely, they'll feel their losses strongly after you arrive and won't "jump in" to the new culture as quickly as you had expected them to.

Reluctance to integrate into the new culture. It may surprise you when the child who was most excited to move is also the one who has the hardest time after you arrive. They may become melancholy, angry, and mildly depressed shortly after you reach your destination, and they may not engage in the new culture as much as you would have anticipated they would. It may take weeks or months before they begin to settle in, and that time can be stressful for parents who are hoping that their children will adjust quickly.

Poor performance in the new school. Starting a new school in a new country is challenging in and of itself, but it is especially so for a post-griever. School is an easy place for them to "see" what they have left behind. They no longer have friends to sit with at lunch, rapport with the teachers, perhaps even a familiar grading system. If they are homeschooling and were attending a school outside the home in the previous country, they may miss the social aspect of going to school. No matter the type of school they are a part of, they may be unable to concentrate well and may not want to engage socially or academically. Like pre-grievers before a move, post-grievers often struggle to excel or meet expectations in school when they first arrive in the new place.

Bad behavior. Children don't understand that they are grieving, and they don't know how to channel the uncomfortable feelings they are experiencing. This often results in anger about the situation and this often manifests in bad behavior. Just like with pre-grievers, it's important to discipline bad behavior but also to have conversations about the grief that is likely the underlying source.

CARING FOR YOUR POST-GRIEVER

If you have a post-grieving child, it can be very easy to become frustrated. You may have expected them to engage and integrate quickly because of their excitement before you left, and that makes it even more challenging when they suddenly change tunes upon arrival. Remember that a key goal in raising TCKs is teaching them to grieve effectively from a young age. This is the perfect scenario to begin that training. So, be patient, give them space, give them time, and let them grieve.

Leaving well is important but arriving well is even more essential for the post-grieving child. When you arrive, encourage them to engage in the new place, but don't push them. Explore, try new foods, do fun family activities, meet people, etc., but also give them space to grieve. Realize that they are processing their new reality and need time and space to do so. Lead by example. Instead of pushing them to get involved, make new friends, and learn the language, start to do so yourself and invite your child along. Give them opportunities to engage, but don't force them to. When they are ready, they will begin to integrate, but they can't and shouldn't do so without first grieving all that they have just lost.

If your child seems to be struggling after arriving overseas, take heart. You likely have a post-griever, and this is the natural and healthy progression they need to go through in order to fully embrace the new place. This season of grief will not end abruptly, but instead will dissipate over time, and before you know it, they will be ready to fully engage in their new life.

EXTREME SADNESS AND DEPRESSION.

For both pre-grievers and post-grievers, it is important to recognize when it is of more serious concern. While sadness is expected and healthy, it is important to know when it turns from sadness to depression.

Signs of depression in children may include:

- self-harm of any kind,
- extreme changes in appetite,
- extreme changes in sleep,
- change in personality,
- abnormal fatigue,
- asking questions about death or suicide,
- feelings of hopelessness, despair, worthlessness.

If you notice any of these symptoms in your child lasting longer than a couple of weeks, it is critical that you seek professional help from someone who can help your child process the grief of the impending move. Grief is healthy and normal, but depression is a serious issue that needs to be addressed promptly.

DRAWING THE LINE FROM GRIEF TO TRAUMA

We'll talk about trauma more in depth in the following chapter, but I want you to see how grief and trauma are incredibly interconnected and the line that can often be drawn from one to the other.

Complex trauma is an area that has recently received a lot of attention from mental health researchers. They have found that this type of trauma does not occur from one traumatic event, but instead, like the Grief Tower, it builds over a period of time when repeated stressful events occur in childhood and are not processed effectively. The symptomatic manifestation of this is Complex Post Traumatic Stress Disorder (C-PTSD).

"C-PTSD sufferers may 'stuff' or suppress their emotional reaction to traumatic events without resolution either because they believe each event by itself doesn't seem like such a big deal or because they see no satisfactory resolution opportunity available to them."[32]

When you experience repeated stress, as many TCKs do, and you don't process it in the moment, your brain gets stuck and at some point, likely years later, you may experience physical symptoms associated with trauma (nightmares, anxiety, depression, headaches, etc.). If it's not dealt with at that point, the manifestations get worse, more intrusive, and more debilitating.

I see this trend happening with many adult TCKs. They seem to do very well in high school and even at university, but then at some point in their mid-twenties they have a breakdown. I have heard countless stories and personally know many adult TCKs who have severe mental health disorders, and those of us working in the TCK world predict that the undercurrent is most often an issue of unresolved grief. If this unresolved grief is prevented, could it also perhaps prevent the development of trauma-related issues? I believe so.

In fact, one of my deepest desires is to see a significant decrease in unresolved grief issues among Third Culture Kids. Parents, organizations, and others with TCKs in their lives have a direct influence on seeing this come to fruition.

Here are some ways to begin resolving grief:

Provide comfort. Comforting is not saying positive things to counteract the grief, but rather, it is sitting with your kids in the midst of their pain. Depending on your children's personalities, the most comforting things can be as simple as a hug, a meaningful gift, or a listening ear. The purpose is not to fix or diminish the grief but to let them know that you care, understand, and desire to validate their feelings.

Be an example. The losses that you have experienced through moving and living overseas may not be the same as those your children have experienced, but you talking about them tells your TCK, "It is okay to be sad about these things!" This is also a great way to spark conversation about the hidden losses. As you are folding your new bedsheets fresh out of the dryer or off the clothes line, you can say, "Sometimes I really miss the sheets I had back in Thailand. Do you ever miss your bed and your old bedroom?" These simple conversation starters tell your child that it is okay to think about these things, talk about these things, and miss these things.

Provide resolution in young adulthood. Often, deep-seated grief does not surface for Third Culture Kids until later into young adult life, most commonly in their late twenties. When their Grief Tower comes crashing down, it often leaves destruction in its wake for both the TCK and the bystanders. In order to avoid this collapse, it is critical that TCKs have a chance to lift blocks off of the tower as early as possible in their young adult lives, and you can be an instrument in this process. This step is perhaps the most key tool in preventing unresolved grief because the TCK is taking the opportunity to sit in, process, work though, and validate the grief and loss that they have experienced up until that point.

The resolution of grief can come in many forms, but it is important to ensure that you are encouraging *processing* grief, not just *diffusing* the negative feelings. There is more on this in the next section. This grief processing could come in the form of deep conversations within your family about the experiences, both positive and negative, of your children's lives overseas.

I recommend creating a grief timeline. Sit with you TCK and have them think through each of the blocks on their Grief Tower. Which was the very first grief-inducing incidence that they can remember? What came after that? It works well to draw a timeline and write these instances in chronological order. Allow them to talk and process through each of them. If they aren't comfortable talking about them with you, encourage them to journal about it or use one of the other processing techniques that I'll address in this chapter.

Their unstacking of the blocks could also happen through counseling, which many universities provide to students at no cost. The counseling should explore all the sources of grief and loss during the child's life in order to process through those well.

It is important that as a family you take the initiative and take the time to revisit and openly process the difficult experiences in your children's lives. This will likely be very beneficial for you as well. It is all too easy to keep moving forward in life without taking the time and energy to rehash the difficult things of the past. It may even feel counterproductive to you to bring up these negative feelings, but in contrast, it is one of the most helpful, healing gifts that you can give your young adult TCKs as they enter into adulthood.

Prioritize your relationship. Processing grief with your TCKs in a healthy way is a critical part of fostering a healthy relationship with them. When you provide them a safe environment to feel the difficult feelings that come with grief and you acknowledge their pain, you open up the door for them to share future hurts with you. The losses that TCKs often experience in their lifetime and their parents' reactions to those losses predict whether or not they will feel safe reaching out to their parents when future grief-inducing experiences occur—particularly in teenage years and adulthood. If they felt invalidated, not comforted, unimportant, ashamed, or foolish because of their parents' reaction to their childhood grief, it is very difficult for parents to prove to them later in life that they are safe people who will now comfort and validate their feelings.

DIFFUSING VERSUS PROCESSING

As I alluded to, there is an important distinction that needs to be made, and that is the difference between *processing* grief and *diffusing* negative feelings. Grief is a complex emotion that is often intertwined with many others like anger, sadness, and fear. In my experience, parents often react to their children's grief-induced emotions and related behavior by diffusing it. They do this by cheering them up when they are sad, disciplining their anger-induced behavior, or reassuring them that there is nothing to fear. These can certainly be good first steps, but often parents don't move from this to the critical next step of processing the root cause: grief. This is especially true with young children who naturally act out behaviorally when faced with negative emotions.

This concept, however, is not just for young children. During a teen TCK training I led several summers ago, the students asked for an additional session on the topic of grief, and they specifically asked if we could talk more in depth about the difference between diffusing and processing. As teens, they were struggling with working through their grief but knew that it was often the source of their angst and anger. I was so glad they were vulnerable enough to push this conversation to that deeper level.

The concepts of diffusing negative emotions and processing grief may look similar and may use similar methods, but they are absolutely not the same. In fact, doing one at the expense of the other can lead to a host of unresolved grief issues, many of which we discussed earlier in this chapter. As a parent or caretaker of TCKs, it is critical that you understand and practice both so that you can also teach your TCKs to understand and practice both.

Here is the difference: diffusing takes your mind off the negative emotions, while processing allows for time to dwell on the negative emotions. Sometimes, it is important to diffuse because processing would not be appropriate in that time and space. However, it is critical that when there is time, processing takes place. Knowing the difference between the two allows this to be a conscious process.

DIFFUSING

Anger is often the bubbling over of deeper, more complex emotions such as loneliness, stress, tiredness, sadness, etc. When your children are acting out in anger, keep in mind that there is very likely a deep, underlying cause for their outbursts. While anger is an allowed and acceptable emotion, there are appropriate ways to express and diffuse that anger. The "Get Out My Angry Cards" I introduced earlier in this chapter are designed to be a diffusing tool. The ideas such as "do jumping jacks, take deep breaths, play outside, read a book, etc." are ideal ways to get your mind off the negative emotions. For young children I always encourage some form of physical activity. Once this diffusing has happened, you can move on to processing the emotions.

PROCESSING

The reason that so many TCKs suffer from issues related to unresolved grief is because they never move from distraction techniques associated with diffusing negative emotions to the more introspective—more difficult—grief processing. They spend their childhoods and young adult lives getting their minds off the negative feelings when they arise and never take the time to dwell on them strategically in order to process through those negative feelings.

Grief processing sounds complex, but it is a simple concept that is just as important and effective for a four-year-old as it is for a sixty-year-old. It is simply allowing yourself to think through the "whys" of your negative emotions. Your young TCKs will need more hands-on help to process these big emotions, while your older TCKs, if given the tools, often desire to process more independently, though it is still critical that you intentionally encourage them in this, as it will not likely happen naturally.

As you help your TCKs to process their grief, take care to allow them to grieve without pointing out the up-side. Therapist Lois Bushong says, "If you attempt to reframe their losses into gains, the result is feelings of shame and withdrawal or anger. If you attempt to defend the system that sent (you) abroad, they will shut down and internalize that you don't understand them. Yes, there are two sides to their experiences and it can be a challenge to embrace both the positive and negative of each of these events. But before they are willing to consider any positives, they have to experience comfort in their world of grief and loss. Ultimately, they will recognize their history is a weaving of gains and losses."[33]

It can be challenging to sit with them in their grief without reframing their losses as gains, but it is an incredibly important part of their grief-processing and your relationship with them through it.

Below are some practical ways to encourage your TCKs to process their grief.

Younger kids:

- Draw a picture of your feelings or the places/things/people you miss.
- Sculpt something that you miss.
- Talk about it.
- Make up a story of a child going through a similar situation, then act it out with your dolls or toys.

Older kids:

- Journal.
- Find a quiet place to sit and reflect.
- Write a song.
- Talk with a friend or parent.
- Pray or meditate on it.
- Take a walk and think.
- Ask yourself questions:
- "What am I feeling right now?" (Sad, lonely, rejected, uneasy, anxious, afraid)
- "Why am I feeling that way?"

The point of grief processing is to take the time to think about the negative emotions, why you feel that way, and whether there is anything that needs to be done to move on. It is not a fun process, and most of us try to avoid those hard, deep feelings, but it is incredibly important. If you are intentional about teaching your TCKs to diffuse their anger, process their grief, and understand the difference between the two while they are young, you will be well on your way to setting them up to be emotionally healthy kids, teens, and adults.

ART AND PLAY FOR GRIEF PROCESSING

As you may have noticed, I often suggest artistic activities for parents and TCKs. There is a good reason for this! In my years of training young TCKs, I have found that artistic outlets are often the best way to get a glimpse of what is going on below the surface, and often yields an entrance for deeper conversations. Art and play not only gives us a window into a child's world but also allows them to enter into their own mind in a way that they would not naturally conjure up—especially in conversation. When they are directed in art and play specifically for grief processing, they seem to realize for themselves thoughts, fears, joys, grievances they didn't know they had or, at the very least, couldn't put into words. This is why I am constantly utilizing this method in my trainings. It helps both myself and the child to recognize their emotions, which allows me to work more effectively with them. I believe the same method can absolutely be applied in your family.

It is important that you, the parent, create structured times so that you can be watchful, attentive, and ready to follow up with your child. The play and art that you have your children do should have an underlying purpose and not simply be "free play" though you may begin to notice themes in their free play time as well.

Here are some examples of activities you can instruct your children to do:

- **Draw** a picture of a time when you felt very happy and draw another picture of a time when you felt very sad.
- **Sculpt** something that makes you feel excited and something that makes you feel scared or nervous when you think about moving (going on furlough, starting a new school, etc.).
- **Create a skit** with your siblings about when we moved to _____ and perform it for us!
- **Draw** some of your favorite things about living here and some things that you miss about your passport country.
- **Choreograph a dance** about how you're feeling right now

(how you felt when we moved, how you feel when you think about moving, how you feel about being a TCK, etc.).

- **Paint** a picture of what your insides feel like right now.
- **Draw** one of your favorite memories of our family.

There are many others that you could think of specific to your family and what your TCKs are currently dealing with. The point is to make it fun, but always have a goal in mind—something to be watching for. A fun idea is to write these and perhaps other ideas on popsicle sticks, place them in a jar, and allow your children to select one to do from the jar. Once your children have created their art, be sure to follow up with the following steps on your part: paying attention and talking about it.

Pay attention. You don't have to be a psychologist to find deeper meaning in what your children display in their art and play. In fact, most children subconsciously *want* their parents to pick up on their deeper feelings; they just don't know how to express them verbally. As your children sculpt, draw, act, dance, or paint, you may notice things that surprise you. For example, when you ask your TCKs to paint a picture of what their insides feel like right now, they may choose dark colors and paint jagged and twisted patterns. You might notice that their insides don't "look" very happy. Older TCKs might draw butterflies, a sign that your TCKs might feel nervous or anxious about something. If your TCKs direct and perform a play about the move overseas, you may be very surprised to see that their perspectives on what took place are very different from yours. When you ask your TCKs to draw one of their favorite memories of your family, pay attention to the country where the memory takes place, the people involved, how long ago it took place, etc. Again, this is not "free play" and isn't something for your TCKs to do quietly on their own. Instead, you should be very attentive, asking questions, looking for things that surprise you, and looking for deeper meaning.

I once had a five-year-old in my program who was moving to the Middle East. I had asked all the kids to sculpt something that they were excited about and something that made them feel nervous or scared when they thought about moving. When they went around the circle to show the sculpture of what they were nervous or scared about, this little boy showed his sculpture of himself in a bed. When I asked what he had sculpted, he smashed his sculpture with his fist and said, "I'm scared I'm going to get bombed in my sleep." Obviously, this was a serious concern, and I was able to address it with his parents who were very surprised as they had never heard him say anything about that. Art and play can bring many things to the surface that might otherwise never be said.

Talk about it. Ask questions about your children's art and play. "Why did you choose those colors?" "That looks kind of scary!" "What is this a picture of?" "What made that your favorite memory?" "Tell me about your sculpture!"

This is where you may have the opportunity to engage in deeper conversations that you may not have had with your TCKs up to this point. Art and play opens up the conversations like nothing else I have found. Take the time to talk with your TCKs about their art and ask elaborating questions. You will likely see and hear things that surprise you. Remember never to disregard or shrug off your child's feelings as this may keep them from sharing them again. Instead say something like, "I didn't realize you felt that way. Those are some big feelings! Let's talk about this some more."

It is important to note that because art and play can bring deep, harbored feelings to light, it is critical that they are taken seriously especially if they indicate thoughts of harm to self or others. If your child seems to focus their art or play on death, destruction, or physical harm of any kind, it may be necessary to seek professional counseling services. If there is nothing available in your area, you may resort to an online option. Unfortunately, I have seen parents shrug off serious concerns, saying, "She doesn't really mean anything by it," or "He's just trying to get attention." Anytime children express thoughts of harm to themselves or others, it needs to be taken very seriously.

Art and play is a wonderful way to help your TCKs express themselves for their own sake as well as yours as a parent. By giving them an outlet, you are helping them to process their complex feelings in a healthy way, and by paying attention to their art and play, you are getting a little window into your child's internal world. What you see and learn from your children during these activities may surprise you and will hopefully open the door for honest conversations between you and your TCKs.

RELATED BENEFITS — EMPATHY:

Grief is an unavoidable part of the TCK life. By giving them the skills and permission to grieve at a young age, they are better equipped for the challenges that are an inevitable part of their experiences. Healthy TCKs who can feel, process, and resolve their grief develop a beautiful ability for empathy, connection, and compassion.

The grief that TCKs experience is difficult, no doubt. However, if it is worked through and preventive practices are put into place, the result is an amazing ability for them to empathize. Empathy is a skill that has significantly decreased in recent generations. A study done by the University of Michigan showed that 75 percent cared significantly less about others than the same demographic thirty years prior. Apathy is increasing in the general population, yet empathy is a skill that Third Culture Kids prominently possess.[34] By proactively caring for their grief, you are empowering them with the increasingly rare skill of true empathy.

THE MAIN IDEAS:

- Frequent good-byes are one of the hardest aspects of the TCK life. Take care to walk through these well as they contribute to the TCK's future relationship-building tendencies.
- Many of the TCK losses are hidden, but unresolved grief can be avoided by bringing them out of hiding.
- Learning how to grieve is critical for TCKs because unacknowledged and unresolved grief can compound and become complex trauma.
- Teach TCKs the difference between grief processing and diffusing negative feelings so that they don't do one at the expense of the other.
- Use art and creative play to help your TCKs process grief and work through difficult emotions.

QUESTIONS TO CONSIDER:

- Does your TCK seem to be a pre-griever or post-griever?
- Are you a pre-griever or post-griever?
- What is one thing you can do today to start proactively helping your TCKs process grief?
- What can you begin to do to model healthy grief-processing for your TCKs?
- How can you implement some of the skills in this chapter during your family check-ins?

CHAPTER 6

Understanding Trauma

Healthy TCKs have addressed and processed the difficulties of their TCK lives and reaped a beautiful resiliency as a result.

I sat in a counselor's office at twenty-three years old. I was there because I had been experiencing horrible nightmares for months. I would wake up yelling and drenched in sweat. My husband finally convinced me to see a therapist.

"This sounds like a reaction to trauma," my therapist said. "Have you experienced any traumatic events?"

"I don't think so," I said.

"Well, maybe start by telling me some of the significant events that you remember about your time in Africa. Things that really stick with you."

I recounted the following events.

The first week that we arrived in Tanzania, we were driving down the road with our driver, Dennis. I looked out the window and saw a crowd and a screaming man being dragged though the dirt and engulfed by the sea of people. Through the crowd, I could see them as they threw a tire over the man, poured gasoline on him, and lit him on fire. I can still remember the smell, hear the screams and the chanting crowd, and feel the horrible, sick feeling in my stomach. I asked Dennis what was going on, and he said, "Oh, he probably stole something. *Kawahida*" (Swahili for "it's normal").

Within the first two years of our time in Tanzania, two close friends of mine died of HIV/AIDS. For one, the final months were long and drawn out; the other died suddenly in her sleep. Both were events that my fourteen-year-old self didn't know how to comprehend. I distinctly remember not crying, not processing, and wondering why I didn't feel anything but numb.

Several years later, I was riding down the road and witnessed a terrible car accident. A van-type vehicle had crashed into a motorcycle and killed the driver. A mob quickly formed, pulled the driver of the van from his seat, and dragged him off to beat him to death—the punishment for a fatal car accident.

I told these stories like they were no big deal while the counselor kept nodding and jotting notes. She looked up. "I think we've identified the source of your nightmares. Now, tell me about moving back from Africa."

Our first move back from Africa was sudden. I didn't have time for many good-byes or to process what was taking place. Most of the people I was closest to I wouldn't see until ten years later, and some I never saw again. We went straight from Africa to a live-in counseling center for three months, and then I began public high school in California. At first I liked being the girl who came from Africa (especially after watching *Mean Girls* for the first time!), but then the novelty wore off, and I was just awkward, lonely, and misunderstood. High school is hard enough, but add in culture stress, anxiety, and unresolved grief and it's the perfect prescription for a horrible experience. Not to mention, that was the year we lived in eighteen different houses.

Up until that point, I had never thought of these events as traumatic. They were just a normal part of African life and transition. No one else seemed to be bothered by these things, so it didn't seem to be anything that I should make a big deal of.

DEFINITIONS

SMALL *T* TRAUMA

"Small 't' traumas are events that exceed our capacity to cope and cause a disruption in emotional functioning. Small 't' traumas tend to be overlooked by the individual who has experienced the difficulty. This is sometimes due to the tendency to rationalize the experience as common and therefore cognitively shame oneself for any reaction that could be construed as an over-reaction or being 'dramatic.'"[35]

Something physically traumatic does not need to happen to TCKs for them to experience deep trauma. Witnessing traumatic events, experiencing intense or sudden loss, and being exposed to extreme poverty are all examples of this small *t* trauma, and one or all of them are likely to be experienced by your TCKs. The challenge is that in Third World countries and in expatriate circles, these events may be so common that the people are desensitized, and the types of events that would be easily considered traumatic elsewhere are just considered to be a normal part of living overseas. I believe this is a critical conversation to have when discussing TCK care.

Most TCKs who suffer from trauma are experiencing the small *t* trauma described above. In other cases, more severe trauma, known as large *T* trauma, may occur.

LARGE *T* TRAUMA

"A large-T trauma is distinguished as an extraordinary and significant event that leaves the individual feeling powerless and possessing little control in their environment. Such events could take the form of a natural disaster, terrorist attack, sexual assault, combat, a car or plane accident, etc. Helplessness is also a key factor of large 'T' traumas, and the extent of experienced helplessness is far beyond that of a small 't' trauma."[36]

For this chapter on understanding trauma, I will be focusing on small *t* trauma, though large *T* traumas do occur in the lives of many TCKs. If you believe your child has experienced large *T* trauma and has not had follow-up mental health care, it is critical that you seek that out as soon as possible.

It is important to be aware that small *t* trauma is not only likely but almost unavoidable during the TCK experience, but that there are ways to keep it from manifesting into anything symptomatic. By being aware that this is a reality, you can strategically help your TCKs to process small *t* trauma in intentional ways that you couldn't possibly if you weren't educated on this issue.

It is also important to understand how the "victim versus survivor" mentality plays into the TCK experience in regard to trauma. One significant challenge that is relatively unique to the TCK experience is the feeling of being trapped in grief-inducing circumstances that are completely out of their control. TCKs often do not have a choice in the decision to move overseas, and sometimes their parents did not have the choice either. An organization, government, company, military agency told the family where they were going to live and when they were going to go, and they simply had to follow orders. For the children, these authority structures are even more ambiguous and can lead to a heavy sense of having no choice or escape in this challenging life they are living. Interestingly, this is one of the main diagnostic requirements of C-PTSD:

> Complex Post Traumatic Stress Disorder (C-PTSD) is a condition that results from chronic or long-term exposure to emotional trauma *over which a victim has little or no control and from which there is little or no hope of escape.*[37]

This can easily lead to a victim mentality for children and teens. They are experiencing difficulties that involve grief and potentially trauma, and they know that there is no way out. They often don't feel like they even have an emotionally safe escape within the countries where they're living. Unlike children who grow up in one culture and live near relatives and longtime friends and have trusted relationships to turn to during challenging times, TCKs face incredibly challenging times and their "safe place" is three airplane rides and two days away. To a young TCK, this can feel incredibly trapping.

PREVENTION

Dr. Mark Rains, a clinical psychologist who specializes in resilience, points out how critical parents are in preventing stressful events from being stored in the brain as trauma and instead becoming a catalyst in resilience building. "Take two children who experience the same stress," Rains explains. "One of them might have a parent who's able to help their response system get back to normal and the other might remain stressed without the support system to help them feel safe again. That chronic stress may lead to toxic effects."[38]

A study conducted on resiliency and recovery following traumatic events identified several factors that prevent toxic stress from developing into trauma as well as prevent long-term side effects of trauma. These factors are:

- continuous contact with and support from important people in your life,
- disclosing the trauma to loved ones,
- identifying as a survivor as opposed to a victim,
- use of positive emotion and laughter,
- finding positive meaning in the trauma,
- helping others in their healing process,
- holding the belief that you can manage your feelings and cope.[39]

The most significant reason that I have found for these prevention elements not occurring in the young TCK's life is because of a lack of acknowledgment by parents, organizations, friends, family, and other caregivers that the TCK's life events were traumatic or grief-inducing. Because so many of the losses in the TCK's life are "hidden," as I discussed in chapter 5, it is easy to think of them as simply a part of the life of an overseas worker. It is also important to note that every person's experience is different—especially when we are considering the difference in perspective of a small child versus an adult. To the parent, the move to a new country may have been difficult, but they would never describe it as traumatic. However, to a seven-year-old it may absolutely be mentally processed and stored as a trauma. I have talked with countless parents, whose adult children are severely struggling, and I bring up this idea of trauma and unresolved grief. The majority of parents will answer,

"But nothing really traumatic happened overseas. We were never robbed, they were never sexually assaulted, they didn't witness any murders." To which I respond, "There may not have been anything traumatic for you, but that doesn't necessarily mean that nothing was traumatic for them."

There is certainly the possibility that a TCK's current struggles are not trauma related, but it is important not to assume that is the case. As you note in the list above, the first two ways to prevent trauma are continuous contact with and support from important people in the TCK's life and disclosing the trauma to loved ones. From my experience working with hundreds of families who have lived overseas, the majority of TCKs do not have this support simply because of the parents' response to their children's struggles. When I talk with TCKs about their lives overseas, I often hear underlying themes of grief and trauma. But when I mention to the parents that trauma and unresolved grief could potentially be the source of their TCKs' struggles, I often get a response like one of the following:

- "I can't believe they even remember that event. It wasn't that big of a deal."
- "We all went through that; it really wasn't that traumatic."
- "They are just exaggerating and trying to get attention."
- "They are using this to excuse their bad choices and behaviors."
- "Our family has been able to do so many awesome things. We've lived an amazing life and had opportunities that most people only dream of. Why are they complaining?"

One of the most significant ways to help TCKs properly process their grief and trauma is to acknowledge their grief and trauma. If they don't feel like you will validate their feelings, they will adopt the belief that they have to push them down, be strong, and look like they are fine. This was my story, and it has not been an easy process to rewrite.

There are far too many adult TCKs who no longer have healthy relationships with their parents because their parents chose not to acknowledge the severity of the trauma they experienced. Perhaps they fall into the category of those who normalize it as a part of the TCK experience or don't want to acknowledge that there could be a very difficult side of a very amazing, incredible life experience.

Unfortunately, ignorance prevents deep relationship. It keeps TCKs from feeling like they have advocates in their parents. There are few things that will cause a TCK (or anyone, really) to shut down emotionally more than sharing something they feel was traumatic only to be told they are exaggerating, overreacting, being dramatic, or being too sensitive. Protect your relationship with your TCKs by affirming their views of their experiences and helping them to process through them in a healthy way.

One easy way for parents to acknowledge trauma or even just minor difficulties that occur is during the family check-in time that I discussed in chapter 2. With this time already set aside, it is convenient to bring up difficult events and process them as a family. The most critical part of this is that if something does happen (a car accident, a robbery, a home invasion, something you noticed that induced fear for your child, etc.), you can bring it up during check-in time. If something obviously scary or difficult happens during the day and parents don't acknowledge it during check-in time, it could communicate to the children that it is taboo to talk about or it is not a big enough deal to bring up.

PROCESSING WITH YOUR TCKS

Parents are often the people witnessing these traumatic experiences along with the children, or at least, they are aware of the events taking place, so they are in an ideal position to help their children process them.

Like I mentioned, children often feel like the difficult things they see are taboo to talk about, or they feel like they shouldn't be affected by them because it looks like everyone else isn't. The message that they receive from the culture around them is, "This is a normal part of life." Thus, it is important that parents are intentional about having these conversations.

Here are some ideas:

As you notice difficult events and occurrences, and especially if your children point them out, make a mental note to talk through them at the end of the day. Often it isn't possible or appropriate to process in the moment, but don't let that keep you from processing. Create the space and time to do so later.

Clearly state the difficult event or scene that you and your child witnessed.

Example 1:
"When we were walking through town today, do you remember seeing the child who was begging for money and didn't have any legs?"

Example 2:

"When we were walking through the market today, there were so many people touching you and grabbing your hair!"

Then, help them to process their emotions of the experience.

Example 1:

"I could see by your face that you were having a hard time looking at him. How did it make you feel to see him there? Do you think he's about the same age as you?"

For younger kids, give them feeling words instead of asking them how they feel.

"I could see by your face that you were having a hard time looking at him. He looked about the same age as you! Did it make you feel sad to see that?"

Example 2:

"It can be really uncomfortable to have so many people touching you and grabbing your hair! Does it scare you or worry you when that happens?"

The point of these conversations is not necessarily to bring resolution but instead to allow them to process what they saw or experienced. By doing so, you keep those things from being planted, amplified, and locked into their brains where they become blocks that stack on their Grief Tower. When you help them to process, you keep the memories from carrying too much mental weight that their young brains can't reasonably process.

I have worked with many parents who were afraid to talk about grief, loss, and trauma for fear of reminding their children of the sad things, bringing up a loss, fear, or event that their children hadn't even thought of, causing their children to wish they weren't TCKs, or causing their children to blame them (the parents), the work they're doing, or God for the challenges. Unfortunately, by not talking about them, parents only enforce the subconscious idea that they are not significant losses or events and instead should be ignored. By bringing them up gently with your children, you can help them to connect their feelings to tangible and valid reasons for those feelings. Many times, TCKs simply need to know that there are legitimate reasons behind their seemingly intangible sadness and thus know that it is okay to be sad.

It is also important for you to provide an example of healthy ways of processing through difficult experiences. When something traumatic happens, do you just continue on with life as usual or do you display some process of working through your emotions of that experience? Do your children see this? This could be as simple as meeting with another family or trusted friend to talk through what happened or taking a spontaneous vacation to do something fun as a family. Remember that play is the antidote to stress!

When something serious and traumatic does occur, it is important for parents to model the seriousness. This often shows up in the parents' willingness to seek help for their own challenging experiences of living overseas. I highly recommend that this be a counselor (many even provide services from a distance) who has experience working with globally mobile families. The International Therapist Directory (www.InternationalTherapistDirectory.com) is a great resource for finding a counselor. Be sure also to find a way to set up a safe place for your TCKs to talk through their experiences.

This could be an online TCK counselor, a trusted teacher, a friend back home whom they can call frequently, older trusted TCKs, etc.

GIVE THEM CONTROL

Allow your child to make decisions where and when possible. This helps them to feel that while everything else in life seems out of their control, there are still some things they can have control over. Let them help make decisions such as choosing curtains or bedding for their room, choosing a paint color for their room, choosing their school, choosing the activities they're involved or not involved in, etc.

GIVE THEM AN ESCAPE

Help them to create an "escape" in their room where they can go when they have big emotions to process. Here are some ideas:

- Let them set up a corner of their room with a beanbag and encouraging posters.
- Let them paint their room whatever color they want.
- Give them a desk in their room where they can journal.
- Let them decorate in a way that feels peaceful and homey to them.
- Set up an art area in their room where they can express their emotions through creativity.

RELATED BENEFITS — EMPATHY AND RESILIENCE:

When TCKs have processed through the difficult elements of their upbringings, two things happen. One, they are able to empathize with others who are dealing with difficult situations and approach their own difficult experiences from a healthy perspective.

Two, they know that they can face difficult things and come out on the other side stronger. They are able to see the challenges that they faced as directly responsible for amazing benefits. They can truly testify to how deep hurt can be redeemed into a beautiful and rich ability to love others well and live a whole and healthy life.

THE MAIN IDEAS:

- TCKs are prone to witnessing traumatic events, experiencing small *t* trauma and sometimes even large *T* trauma.
- The negative, long-lasting effects of trauma can be prevented by parents acknowledging traumatic situations, processing them with your TCKs, and being an emotionally safe person for them.
- Have conversations with your TCKs when difficult events and experiences take place. This prevents those instances from being stored in the brain as trauma.
- Create an escape where your TCKs can go to process difficult things.

QUESTIONS TO CONSIDER:

- Have any events occurred in your overseas experience that could have been experienced as traumatic by your children?

- If you have yet to process those experiences, how can you do that as a family?
- What was the most difficult thing in this chapter for you to read and think about?

CHAPTER 7

Anchoring the TCK's Identity

Healthy TCKs have pieces of their identity that remain anchored while they skillfully adapt to the cultures around them.

Identity is bred and fostered in belonging and belonging fosters resilience.

The reason the discussion about TCK identity and belonging is so important is not only because we want our TCKs to have a healthy view of self and connection within a group but also because those things yield resilience. The TCK life is one that requires an intense level of resilience.

In a study on resilience, it was found that a sense of belonging in the family and community is a key factor in being resilient and is a predictor of success socially and academically in adulthood.

FEELING MISUNDERSTOOD

Researcher Brené Brown tells us that "The greatest barrier to true belonging is fitting in or changing who we are so we can be accepted."[40] Changing who they are so that they can be accepted is a survival skill that Third Culture Kids master. This is a helpful technique when hopping from culture to culture, but at some point, often as young adults, they realize that they have rarely felt like they truly belong and are understood without the effort of working to fit in.

Dr. Brown asked a large group of eighth graders to explain the differences between fitting in and belonging. Some of their answers were:

- "Belonging is being somewhere where you want to be, and they want you. Fitting in is being somewhere where you really want to be, but they don't care one way or the other."
- "Belonging is being accepted for you. Fitting in is being accepted for being like everyone else."
- "I get to be me if I belong. I have to be like you to fit in."[41]

Third Culture Kids are masters at fitting in but rarely feel this sense of belonging—especially when they are back in their passport countries. In Brown's study, she also found that having a sense of belonging at home is the most important space to belong. Because TCKs can feel so different from their parents, many feel they don't even belong in their own family. They may feel misunderstood, not liked, embarrassed, not successful, not worthy of attention, etc.

In her research on TCKs, Tanya Crossman found that one third feel misunderstood by their parents. This greatly impacts their identity formation as they grow into adulthood. While a lack of belonging and identity confusion may be present when TCKs are children and teenagers, these issues are most likely to creep up and declare themselves when TCKs are adults and are living through the years when the most significant identity formation takes place (ages 22–35). During this time period the majority of TCKs are no longer living in the countries in which they grew up, and they are beginning careers, navigating relationships, having children of their own, and developing adult friendships.

When it comes to belonging, TCKs are a lot like fish. Bear with me, this is going somewhere.

Being a Third Culture Kid is a lot like swimming in a school of fish. The fish all innately know which direction to go, when to turn, when to swim up, when to swim down, and they move beautifully and flawlessly together. When the TCK enters a group that all belong to the same passport culture, they are like a fish entering a school of fish. Because they are excellent at reading situations and adapting so that they look like they belong, they look to the other fish and onlookers like they are part of the group. What the others don't know is how much mental energy it is taking for the TCK to look like they belong. With each change in direction, the TCK is anxiously scurrying to keep up while making sure no one notices their effort. It is exhausting!

It takes a very long time for a TCK to be in one place long enough as an adult to truly feel, not just look, like they belong and can swim with the group without putting so much thought into it. Until a Third Culture Kid lives in one place for a significant period of time in their adult life, they are likely to feel a lot like the fish who looks to be part of the school but instead feels a strong lack of belonging within that group.

Like many challenges that TCKs face, this subject of identity and belonging can be addressed proactively throughout the TCK's life. Not only does fostering a healthy identity and a sense of belonging have many positive impacts on their childhood, but it sets them up for greater success in this area when they are adults and encounter a more significant struggle with the issue.

It is important as a parent of TCKs to understand the elements that contribute to the development of the TCK's identity. While there are many more factors involved in an individual's identity make-up, these are the ones that I have found are unique to TCKs and thus are important to discuss and be aware of:

- The Family Identity
- The TCK Identity
- The National Identity
- The Ever-Adapting Identity
- Fear of Losing the TCK Identity
- Not Enough of Any Identity
- Terminal Uniqueness

THE FAMILY IDENTITY

One of the first things I discuss in my workshops on identity is the idea of creating a family identity. A study done at Emory University on family identity revealed the critical nature of having a solid feeling of belonging within the family unit and the effects that this has on a child's self-confidence and resilience. The study showed that, "the ones [children] who knew more about their families proved to be more resilient, meaning they could moderate the effects of stress."[42]

One of the primary ways to combat toxic stress and high-stacked grief tower is to give TCKs a deep sense of belonging in their family. Creating a family mantra, family rules, and family traditions are very practical ways that you can begin doing this in your home.

FAMILY MANTRA

A family mantra is a short statement of your family's purpose and values. For example, "Our family seeks to love and serve each other and those in the community around us."

Dr. Meg Meeker, a pediatrician and parenting expert, says that having a mission for your family to rally behind gives children a sense of *purpose* within the family. It shows them that they *belong* and are a part of the team.[43]

Purpose and *belonging* are trigger words for many TCKs because they touch a deep part of them that yearns to belong and have a clear purpose within a group.

When families move overseas, the children can sometimes feel a lack of purpose—a sense that they are not needed or have no significant role. They feel they are just tagging along with their parents and have no purpose of their own.

They also often experience a lack of belonging. After living overseas, they realize that they don't completely fit into their passport countries anymore, but they are also still foreigners in their host countries. The questions "Who am I?" and "Where do I belong?" resound.

Feeling a sense of belonging and purpose within the family is a critical component to a child's developmental process.

"Belonging lays the foundation for a strong and resilient sense of self – a self which can be sustained through transitions into the wider world and through subsequent experiences that may be less affirming and inclusive."[44]

This "strong and resilient sense of self" is a key component of a healthy adult TCK identity. By being intentional about giving your TCKs a sense of purpose and belonging within the family unit, you are helping to lay that foundation. Creating a family mantra is a great, simple way to begin that process.

Here's how to create a family mantra:

1. **Hold a family meeting and explain what you are trying to accomplish.**
   Example: "We want our family to live overseas as a team and for us to have a united purpose that we can all work on together."

2. **Brainstorm your family's values. Simply start listing them out loud and writing them down.**
   Example: Respecting each other, loving our neighbors, being responsible, being kind, etc.

3. **Work together to turn it into a one or two-sentence statement.**
   Example: "Our family mantra is to love and respect one another and our neighbors, to practice responsibility, and to be kind to everyone around us."

4. **Put it on the wall.**
   Write your mantra and put it in a frame, on a bulletin board, on the bathroom mirror—somewhere where you all can see it.

5. **Implement it!**
   This exercise is pointless if you don't put it into practice. Remind each other of it as you go throughout your days.

The family mantra can be a great tool for any family, but it is particularly valuable for families living overseas. TCKs need to know that they have a purpose and that they belong, and inside the family unit is a great place for that to be instilled in them.

FAMILY RULES

Part of being a member of any system is adhering to the rules. When the cultural systems constantly change in a child's life, it is important for them to know that their family's rules don't change.

A colleague of mine is Korean and moved to the United States with her parents at age thirteen. In Korean culture it is respectful to listen quietly when someone else is speaking and to take a long, silent pause before responding. In her family home it was expected that this rule was upheld in conversations with her parents, despite living in a culture where quick and confident replies were valued. While in school, she learned to raise her hand in class and answer questions quickly, but when she returned to her home each evening, she would adhere to her family's ways of communicating respect.

The rules in your house should be one of the few things that don't change no matter the culture you are living in. Here are some examples of family rules that parents I have worked with have developed:

1. Be kind to everyone.
2. Always obey Mom and Dad.
3. Show respect to your elders.
4. Always tell the truth.
5. Clean up after yourself.
6. Always do your best.

Create a document that lists the rules and keep it in a place where you can all see it—perhaps next to your family mantra! Whenever your children are disciplined or corrected, refer to the family rule that they are breaking. Use phrases like "In our family we . . ." or "You are a Wells, and in the Wells family we . . ."

Family rules teach your children that their identities within your family are an important part of who they are and give them unity and belonging. They also eliminate some of the confusion that can come from living in between cultures. When they know what is expected in the culture of your home, it provides stability and routine that remain consistent despite the expectations of the cultures around them.

FAMILY TRADITIONS AND RITUALS

Family traditions and rituals are often a special part of a child's upbringing, but they serve more purposes than simply being a nice addition to a family's routine, especially for TCKs. Traditions connect TCKs to their larger, intergenerational family even if they no longer live on the same continent as their extended family. Rituals encourage family unity, consistency, and can provide much needed stability, especially during times of transition.

TRADITIONS

Having a sense of family identity through traditions can be very grounding for TCKs. Some family traditions teach TCKs about their passport heritage, such as celebrating a holiday that is native to their passport country and connect them to the past generations of their family. Going back to the Emory University study, "Dr. Duke said that children who have the most self-confidence have what he and

Dr. Fivush call a strong "intergenerational self." They know they belong to something bigger than themselves."[45] This comes from developing an understanding and sense of ownership to their family heritage and realizing that they are part of their family's narrative.

Traditions can be an excellent gateway into teaching your children about their heritage and encouraging knowledge of their family line, thus instilling a sense of belonging within it.

The word "tradition" implies that it is something that needs to happen in the same way, in the same place, but this is not usually possible for globally mobile families. I'd like to suggest that you look for ways to keep traditions that have been passed down through your family no matter which country you are currently in. Though you may need to creatively modify for your location it is often possible to recreate them in some way. This continuity provides a sense of stability and connectedness for TCKs and, amid over-whelming unsettledness, there is a great comfort that comes with knowing that there are some things that are a part of "our family" that will not change.

Traditions also build a bank of positive family memories which are key players in identity development and in encouraging stability in TCKs. When TCKs have good, concrete family memories to look back on, they are less likely to struggle significantly with identity issues and are more likely to be willing to settle down, in some areas of life, when the time comes. Creating memories also leaves a legacy. If your family has celebrated the same heritage holiday each year, your children are likely to continue that tradition with their own families one day, connecting their own children to the family narrative.

You may also consider creating new family traditions. These can be unique to your family or perhaps you will adopt the celebration of local holidays into your family's traditions – adding ties to the cultures you're a part of to your family's narrative. Your children will be able to continue those traditions even if and when they no longer live in that place, which may help them to keep a sense of connectedness to each place they have lived.

RITUALS

Family rituals can be a great antidote for the added stress and tension that many families encounter while living overseas. These happen frequently (daily, weekly, or monthly) and give structure to your children's lives. This can be especially helpful during times of transition and is particularly critical for young children who often respond viscerally to big changes.

I want to highlight one ritual in particular because of the vast research on the benefits. A new organization founded in 2020, *The Family Dinner Project,* has compiled the research done over the years on the differences between families who do or don't eat dinner together regularly. The benefits of family dinners are astonishing.

Families who eat dinner together have:

- Better academic performance;
- Higher self-esteem;
- Greater sense of resilience;
- Lower risk of substance abuse;
- Lower risk of teen pregnancy;
- Lower risk of depression;
- Lower likelihood of developing eating disorders;
- Lower rates of obesity[46]

Because TCKs are already prone to challenges like low self-esteem, substance abuse, and depression this is a critically important ritual to implement in your family. I believe this is one of the simplest and most effective ways to be proactive about raising healthy TCKs.

Growing up, family dinners were valued. We ate around the table together each night even when one parent was traveling. The first evening in our house after moving back to Africa, we had no furniture – only what we had brought in our suitcases and bins. For several nights that week, we ate dinner using a bin for a table, African fabric for a tablecloth, and pillows for chairs. We wouldn't let the lack of table get in the way of our family dinner and we have fun memories to look back on because of it.

It is important to note that rituals don't need to be all or nothing. Expatriate life does not always cater to routine. Prioritize following through with your rituals, like family dinners, but don't fall into guilt and shame when it can't happen or doesn't happen in an ideal way. If your spouse travels often, keep implementing the rituals without them there. If you are in the midst of transition and don't have a dinner table, create a makeshift one. There are ways to continue your rituals through nearly every circumstance if that is a priority and if they have to drop further down priority list for a season, that is ok.

Here's how begin creating family traditions and rituals:

> **Talk about values.** This should be your starting point. Sit down with your spouse and talk about the values that you want to instill in your TCKs. Brainstorm how you can do this through rituals and traditions. For example, if a value is creating quality family time, consider having a "family

night" on a specific day each week. Keep that night free for time to be spent together as just the nuclear family. If you value reading the Bible together, set time aside to do so each evening. If teaching your TCKs about their heritage is important, find ways to celebrate those cultural holidays. Let your rituals and traditions be dictated by your values.

Decide on daily/weekly rituals. These could be starting regular family dinners (or another meal of the day!), starting nightly family check-ins, having the same "fun meal" every Friday night such as pizza or tacos, having pie and movie night on Sundays, etc. The possibilities are endless. The trick is to ensure that you are able to maintain the rituals you choose no matter which country you are in. Consistent daily/ weekly rituals are critical to providing that sense of stability for your TCKs. If you have people staying with you or coming over during the time your ritual would be taking place, invite them to join in! This enhances the identity for your TCKs by allowing them to show others, "This is who we are."

For as long as my husband can remember, his family has been doing "Friday night pizza night." It has morphed with the seasons, but it always includes homemade pizza dough, creative toppings, plenty of wine, and an open invitation to friends and family. He grew up always have a house full of friends and family on Fridays. We have continued this tradition in our family and love that our friends know that they can always show up at our house for pizza if they don't have plans on a Friday night. I hope this Wells tradition is one that passes down to our kids as well.

Plan out holiday traditions. If you plan to celebrate a heritage holiday with specific cultural foods and/or decor, make sure you plan ahead. Stock up on the items you will need and take them with you when you move overseas or ask visitors to bring those items out if they are coming around the time of that holiday. You can also create a new tradition of celebrating the heritage holiday with host-country flare! Find ways to use local ingredients and decor to create your own version of that holiday celebration. Again, this is great for fostering your TCK's identity by showing them that their identity can be comprised of a combination of multiple cultures.

The point of creating rituals and traditions is deeper than simply filling your schedule and creating a routine. They should point to the values that are important to your family, as that will naturally foster your TCK's identity, create a sense of stability, foster resilience, and create memories and traditions that they can pass down to their own children one day.

THE TCK IDENTITY

Many, including myself, struggle with labels and the boxes that they can put people in. I dislike that assumptions are made about individuals simply based on the category they are a part of. Because of this, I completely understand where people are coming from who push back on the idea of labeling TCKs as such.

However, I have seen that, just like most anything else, it can be used well or not well. I love that in the explanation of the TCK definition in *Third Culture Kids 3rd Edition*, the authors explicitly explain that TCKs are people and that each individual will have their own unique experience.[47]

With this individuality in mind, we can then look at common trends among TCKs to give a helpful window into this population's life experience while still giving a lot of room for each TCK to be very different from another.

There are two reasons why the TCK identity is an important piece in a TCKs life. It offers a place of belonging and a roadmap.

The TCK identity can allow for a great and deep sense of belonging with others who share the same label—to the point where many express not feeling as deep a sense of belonging anywhere else. To reject that label, and consequently to reject the group association, can create an even larger gap for TCKs in the area of belonging. As the students in Dr. Brown's study said, "I get to be me if I belong. I have to be like you to fit in." Those of us who are a part of and work in the world of TCKs cannot deny that one of the best (and sometimes only) places where TCKs can say, "I get to be me, *and* I belong," is among other TCKs. When I taught a group of college-age TCKs recently, I joked that I really just came for selfish reasons—so that I could hang out with other TCKs. While I said it in jest, it speaks to a hint of truth—in that place, with other TCKs, I get to be me, and I belong.

Associating with the TCK identity also provides a roadmap. By recognizing that you are a part of a group, you can then look at the general trends associated with that group and process through which are true for you and your life and which may not be. You can also actively prevent common issues and capitalize on common benefits. It's like having a map that shows Point A (the first cross-cultural move) and Point B (a healthy adult TCK). On the map between Point A and Point B are many stops that represent possible challenges and triumphs. Knowing general trends among TCKs shows which stops are most frequently visited by TCKs. This can help those who are proactive about their trip from Point A to Point B avoid the common negative stops and try to hit more of the positive stops. It can also help those who are raising and supporting TCKs to help them navigate this crazy map.

The TCK identity can create belonging among those who have shared in similar life experiences and it can open the eyes of TCKs to a greater awareness of what the challenges and benefits are of this life and how to navigate them well.

THE NATIONAL IDENTITY

A family is back in the United States on home assignment for a year. The six-year-old girl and her parents attend her school's beginning-of-the-school-year assembly. The assembly begins, and everyone stands up to say the Pledge of Allegiance. The girl looks up at her parents and asks, "Mommy, what are we doing?" Her mom's heart sinks.

A TCK returns to England for college after spending the majority of his life overseas. He attends a rugby game, and all of a sudden someone begins to sing a song. "This is strange," he thinks. Stranger still, it appears as though everyone around him knows the words. He mumbles something so it's not obvious that he isn't joining in. "I really should know the words to this," he thinks.

When a child becomes a TCK, they become a global citizen. This is an amazing attribute, but it can leave many parents and family members a bit frustrated and disappointed, as this viewpoint often comes across as a lack of patriotism for the child's passport country. Unlike their parents who may be patriotically tied to one country, TCKs don't typically have ties to a singular country, and if they do, it may not be to their parents' country. This apparent lack of patriotism can create rocky ground for both the TCK and their parents. It can be tricky for parents to understand that, while they have been living overseas just as long as their children have, the impact will be profoundly different for their children than it is for them. The parent who was born and raised in one country may have a difficult time when their TCK does not feel as connected to their passport country.

I like to use the image of a tree to explain this. Picture two trees planted in soil and imagine that you can see the roots beneath the soil. One tree is large and has dense, deep roots that have grown down into the ground. The other tree is small and has sparse, shallow roots. The large tree represents the parent, the small tree represents the child, and the soil represents the culture you are in. When you move overseas, it is like moving those trees to new soil. The large tree will certainly grow some new roots, but they will be shallower and fewer than the roots grown in their home culture. When the child moves, however, they grow their larger, deeper roots of their developmental years in a culture different from their parents' culture. This is why the TCK experience is different from that of an adult who moved overseas.

Here are some things for you to keep in mind as you navigate your TCKs' geographical identities:

Teach your children about their *heritage*, not their *home*. I use the word "heritage" because for the TCK, the passport country of their parents may not feel like their home. By talking about your native country as "home," you may inadvertently cause your TCK to tune out. Make it a point to teach your children about where you (the parents) are from. Teach them about things like traditions, culture, history, food, and holidays, but approach the topic from a heritage perspective. Your children may learn to appreciate that place more if they don't feel like you are trying to convince them that your native country *should* feel like home.

Don't expect them to feel comfortable in your own passport country. When you visit your passport country, remember that while it may be your home, it may not be your child's home. I have talked with many TCKs who had a hard time when they visited their passport countries because their parents seemed to expect them to feel comfortable and jump right back into life in their passport cultures. Your children may not be aware of cultural norms and societal expectations, which can make them feel very out of place. Be mindful of this, and patiently give your TCK space while they (re)adjust to their passport culture.

Don't make them choose a favorite. Often TCKs feel like they have an expected loyalty to their passport country and that given the choice they *should* choose that country over any other. A TCK I know once told me, "One of the worst things I can imagine is my passport country going to war with my host country. I have no idea which country I would side with, and worse, it probably wouldn't be the country my parents would side with, and that would be incredibly shameful." Intentionally reiterate to your TCKs that they can love different places for what each place uniquely has to offer. They don't have to choose a favorite.

When TCKs don't feel like they have to choose an allegiance toward a certain country, they can openly celebrate all the countries they have ties to, and this is an absolutely beautiful part of their TCK identity. As parents, you have the wonderful opportunity and responsibility to be instrumental in shaping how your children view different cultures and people groups. Encourage your children's appreciation of all places, advocate for their global patriotism, and remind them that while every culture has its weaknesses, they also all have something wonderful to offer.

AN EVER-ADAPTING IDENTITY

As you spend time in a particular place, you begin to "catch" the culture that you're in. TCKs become good at this: easily adapting like a chameleon in order to blend into the current environment. As we move from place to place, culture to culture, some things stick around and take up a more permanent residence in our deep root system, shaping values, thought patterns, and ideas. The longer a person lives somewhere, the more likely it is that those deep parts of culture will soak into them and become a part of who they are as a person.

It wasn't until after my first child was born that I began to recognize this ever-adapting identity in myself.

"Who are *you*?" The question was asked during a mom's group I attended when my firstborn was just a couple of months old. The speaker went on, "Not what roles do you play? Not who do people say you are? But who are *you*? If all those roles were stripped away, who would *you* be?" The question sank in and my mind started racing.

Again, TCKs are great at fitting in and not so familiar with belonging.

TCKs become so skilled at morphing into who they need to be to fit in to the given situation that they end up at risk of losing grip on who they actually *are*.

Who am I? What really drives me? Not what have I been told I am? Or what do my roles and location require me to be? But what is just *me*?

Your TCK's adapting nature is an incredible asset, but it is critical that they also keep in mind who they are underneath the TCK role.

Help them to think through which things others say or imply they should be or do or enjoy versus who they have been uniquely created to be. Their ever-changing environment, shifting roles, and TCK identity will absolutely play into who they become as adults. But it is critical that they know who they are at the core so they can separate their foundational self from their ever-adapting self. Nurture your TCK's identity so that their core remains anchored even while the rest of them plays the role of the master adapter.

IDENTITY ANCHOR EXERCISE

This is a great activity for you to do together with your TCK. Create an anchor of your own alongside them, and talk through each other's creation. This can also be an excellent activity for the whole family to do together during a family check-in.

Draw an anchor on a piece of paper or download the worksheet at tcktraining.com/worksheets.

Ask them the following questions. Younger kids may need more assistance coming up with their answers.

- What things do you enjoy doing?
  Examples: playing an instrument, climbing trees, reading books
- What are some character traits that you have?
  Examples: I am kind, I am a good friend, I am patient.
- What are the most important things to you?
  Examples: my family, traveling

Have them write each of their responses inside the anchor. Once you have done this, have them talk though the idea that these things are core to who they are. These are the things that do not and should not change no matter where in the world they are. Perhaps they have to be modified depending on the location, but they are aspects of their identity that should remain anchored even while they may move among different cultures.

FEAR OF LOSING THE TCK IDENTITY

When TCKs realize that they belong to this large group, they often fiercely hold onto that label. For many it is in the TCK group that they first feel like they truly fit in. It is interesting, but if TCKs grow into adults and aren't living an expatriate life, they begin to shed some of their TCK nature, and this process can be scary since the TCK label was defining for them for so long.

For me this began to happen about six years ago when my husband and I moved to Portland, Oregon. Before this, three years was the longest period of time I had lived in one place since elementary school. It was scary to surpass that and not have an intended move on the horizon.

As I began to settle into life here, a deep, unknown fear surfaced: the fear of becoming less of a TCK.

When we decided to buy a house, I could only think, "But TCKs don't do this!" I would remind myself that we were calling it a "five-year house" and could go anywhere in the world after that (even though five years still seemed like a ridiculously long time). Part of me felt like the purchase of our house signaled the death of part of my TCK identity.

Shortly after buying our house, my husband and I were at a craft fair and found a little wooden sign that said Home with the *O* in the shape of Oregon. Something inside me said, "You need to buy this. You are learning to settle." So we purchased the sign and it now sits on a shelf in our living room. Every time I look at it, I feel a slight pang of guilt. "TCKs don't have a home. *Especially* not one in their passport country. I am losing my TCK self."

David Pollock and Ruth Van Reken say, "While parents may change careers and become former international business people, former missionaries, former military personnel, or former foreign service, no one is ever a former Third Culture Kid. TCKs simply grow into being adult Third Culture Kids because their roots grow out of the lives planted in and watered by the third culture experience."[48]

It has been a process for me to learn that I need to let go of *some* of my TCK identity—the part that says, "You will always be rootless," "You will never have a home," "You will never have deep friendships with non-TCKs." I have had to learn that allowing myself to settle here in Oregon is not betraying my TCK self, nor does it make me less of a TCK. In fact, as I look around my house, I can see fingerprints of my overseas upbringing in so many places: my world map on the wall, my cupboards full of African foods and Indian spices, my African-themed guest room, the shuka cloth (Maasai fabric) that I take as a play mat/picnic blanket/towel/blanket for nearly every outdoor activity, African carvings and books in Swahili all around my living room. My third culture experience has played a role in shaping the way that I think, the things that I enjoy, the areas that I am passionate about, and what I want to spend my life pursuing, and is even the reason this book is in your hands.

As you raise and care for TCKs, remember that while being a TCK is a significant part of their identity, it is not all of who they are, nor do they need to hold tight to all that the TCK identity contains. Many teenagers who find out they are TCKs feel a great sense of relief, as I did, as they discover an explanation for so many of their characteristics. As they grow older, however, and assimilate into a new culture (typically when they head off to university), they have trouble finding the balance between shedding some parts of their TCK identity while still holding onto the pieces that are an important part of who they are.

As a parent or someone supporting TCKs, this is something that you can help them walk through as they grow and mature by bringing awareness to this challenge.

NOT ENOUGH OF ANY IDENTITY

Because TCKs have grown their deep roots in a culture (or many cultures) different from that of their parents, they can often feel like they don't identify completely with any. Or, if they do, the people of that culture don't identify them that way. In my own experience, I looked like I should identify with American culture because of my looks and language, but I really identified heavily with African culture. However, in Africa, it was clear from my pale skin that I was not African. I felt I could never be enough of either culture.

This is a common experience for TCKs. Their roots have grown in a wonderful blend of cultures, and it can be difficult to feel like they aren't primarily one. They will never be in one location and feel that they totally belong and share a common identity with that culture (except with other TCKs who share in their blended roots).

TERMINAL UNIQUENESS

Like I talked about in the school of fish analogy, TCKs can sometimes feel like the fish who can't quite swim with the school when they are back in their passport country. They just don't quite fit in with everyone else but can't figure out why – they look like them, they share a passport country. When they finally realize they are a TCK—or, sticking with the analogy, part of a different school of fish—they often respond in one of two ways.

Some TCKs rebel. They want everyone to know, "I *do not* and *will not* fit in!" "I AM NOT PART OF THIS GROUP OF FISH!" They find their way into the other crowds of misfits. Often those crowds are the troublemakers—the anti-conformists who rebel against the rules of society and their parents.

Others prefer to attempt to blend in as stealthily as possible. For me this meant not talking much, wearing neutral colors that were sure not to attract attention, and watching closely in order to swim strategically, hoping to fool people into thinking that I had always been a part of that group.

While most TCKs encounter this experience at some point in their lives and eventually overcome it, for some it evolves into a more serious, long-term identity issue: terminal uniqueness.

I first heard the term "terminal uniqueness" in a college

psychology class. My heart seized up a little. "I know that feeling," I thought. Thankfully, by God's grace, I overcame that challenge in the years between then and now. There are two things that happen when you feel terminally unique:

1. You resolve that you will never fit in, never belong, and never be understood.
2. You judge those who don't share in your uniqueness (aren't TCKs) and decide that you didn't really want to be like "them" anyway.

This dilemma typically arises in high school or college or whenever the TCK returns to their passport country for an extended period of time. Unfortunately, I have observed many TCKs who, as adults, still feel terminally unique. They feel that they will never *really* belong in that group of fish and defensively decide that those fish really aren't worth fitting in with anyway. This strange combination of poor self-esteem mixed with arrogance becomes a stumbling block for far too many TCKs. When the uniqueness truly becomes terminal, it can be incredibly debilitating.

Here are some conversation starters that address and prevent terminal uniqueness:

Unique is not better. TCKs have a stigma of being arrogant. This is an unfortunate but sometimes true reality, and it most often comes into play when the TCK moves back to their passport culture. They realize they are different and have had significantly different life experiences than others their age who are not TCKs. It is easy for them to conclude that their upbringing was superior. Be intentional about fostering humility in your TCKs from a young age and reinforcing that there are benefits and challenges of *any* lifestyle (living in one place, moving around, living overseas, etc.).

TCKs are individuals. TCKs so often get pigeonholed into a category that they begin to forget that they are individuals outside the TCK label. While it is important to address and focus on TCK challenges (especially during the high school and college years), it is equally as important to continue to remind your TCKs that they are unique individuals who have talents and skills, likes and dislikes, and personal opinions and struggles that may or may not be related to their overseas upbringing. Being a TCK absolutely has an impact on who they are, but it is not all of who they are. If your TCK feels too tied to their TCK identity, this can be a recipe for terminal uniqueness because they forget that they are simply a person like everyone else.

TCKs are human. TCKs who feel terminally unique often also feel subhuman. They forget, or decide not to believe, that there are similarities between themselves and others who have lived a different lifestyle. They have a strong "us versus them" mentality and unfortunately often miss out on making what could be amazing friendships because they believe that they are so fundamentally different from "them" that they could never truly be friends.

Give it time. TCKs are inherently good at adapting to new cultures and situations but seem to have a more difficult time using this skill when returning to their passport country. I have found that those who feel terminally unique are often subconsciously surprised when they didn't adapt to their passport country as easily and quickly as they have to the other cultures they have lived in. Because of this, they conclude that they never will fit in and they give up on trying. They isolate, stop trying to make friends, and sadly often resort to unhealthy coping mechanisms to deal with their loneliness. Address your TCK's subconscious expectation that they will quickly jump into life and relationships in their passport culture and continually remind them, "It takes time, stick it out, keep spending time with that potential friend, don't give up!"

Making the decision to live overseas *does* mean that your children will likely feel like misfits in their passport culture, but this challenge doesn't have to be debilitating. In fact, this challenge can be an incredible growing experience.

TCKs who have learned to live successfully in their passport culture have a deep understanding of who they are as a person, have learned to take a stance of humility, and have learned to invest patiently in relationships with people who are not TCKs.

RELATED BENEFITS — BEAUTIFULLY COMPLEX IDENTITY:

While it is difficult for TCKs to feel like they don't completely fit in any place, this mixture of identity influencers allows for a beautifully complex identity. It is always amazing to me how many layers TCKs have to them. This complicated make up becomes an asset as it lays the foundation for why they can adapt so well, develop diverse friendships, and build bridges between people of different cultures. If their identity wasn't so complex, they would never be able to see the world from so many different perspectives.

THE MAIN IDEAS:

- The TCK identity is complex, and it is important that the various components are intentionally fostered.
- Prioritize developing a strong family identity by creating a family mantra, family rules, and family traditions.
- Introduce TCKs to the TCK identity while keeping in mind that they are unique individuals.
- Allow TCKs to identify patriotically with a country as much or as little as they desire. Avoid communicating through thought or action that they are supposed to love one place more than another.
- They may attach to the TCK identity so much that they fear losing it. Talk with them, especially when they are teenagers, about the parts that are healthy and the parts that perhaps they should let go of as adults.
- Have conversations that address and prevent terminal uniqueness—a common TCK identity challenge.

QUESTIONS TO CONSIDER:

- What does your TCK consider to be the defining elements of their identity?
- What are your expectations of your TCK in the area of patriotic identity? Is there any shifting in your thinking that needs to be done?
- How can you communicate with your TCK your love for their global identity?

CHAPTER 8

Engaging in the Culture

Healthy TCKs accept that they are a blend of cultures and places and can claim, and relish in, an integrated life.

O ur first home in Africa was in a small neighborhood called Sakina. We lived in a modest concrete house alongside a handful of other homes like ours and many mud homes. While I attended an international school for the first year we lived there, the majority of my free time was spent out in our neighborhood. My brother and I would walk down the dirt roads to buy eggs from the neighbor's chicken, and another neighbor would bring us a glass jar of fresh milk from his cow each morning. I spent my days playing with the neighborhood kids—learning to speak Swahili through games of charades. I was taught by the village mamas how to cook Tanzanian food, how to make proper Chai, and how to wash clothes by hand. I engaged in daily village life, and before long I was accepted as a local. Outsiders would walk through the neighborhood and say, "*Mzungu!*" ("White person!"), and the neighbors would say very matter-of-factly, "Ah-ah. Lauren *Ni Mswahili*" ("No, no. Lauren is Tanzanian"). By deeply integrating into the culture, I learned a new and different way of living. I learned to befriend and be loved by people who had very different life stories and spoke a different native language. I learned how to live life slowly or, in Swahili, *pole pole* (po-lay, po-lay).

One of the best ways to maximize the benefits of the TCK life is by engaging in the culture you are in. It can be easy to want to stay in the more comfortable expat community if that is an option, but consider the potential benefits of choosing to be deeply involved also in the local culture. This increases your child's love for diversity, adaptability, and language diversity, and enhances all the other benefits of being a Third Culture Kid.

I was listening to an expat podcast recently about raising children overseas. The host was answering questions that had been sent in to her by parents living abroad. A mom wrote in and asked, "What can I do to make sure that my kids stay American while we're living in Europe?" She went on to say that she and her husband wanted their children not to feel "different" when they move back to the USA in a couple of years and thus want to be sure to keep them from adapting too heavily to European culture.

The host provided a myriad of ways that they could "keep their children American." The ideas included making sure to celebrate all American holidays, spending time only with American friends, and not allowing them to learn the local language.

It's a good thing this was a prerecorded podcast because if not, I probably would have called in to offer, very emphatically, a quite different perspective. My response would go something like this and applies to families from any passport country:

1. **You cannot prevent your children from becoming TCKs.** By choosing to live overseas, you have chosen for them to be no longer solely American. No matter how hard

you try to "keep" them American, they will still soak up parts of the culture that you are now living in. Because you are living overseas during their developmental years, this is not preventable. Trying to counteract this natural process will only create problems.

2. **Trying to keep your children from becoming a part of the culture they are living in is unhealthy.** By trying to keep them American, you are teaching them that there is only one right way to do things, that the American way is the best way and any other way of living life is wrong. This leads to a very ethnocentric mind-set and definitely doesn't promote a love and appreciation for diversity.

3. **Why would you want to?** Living overseas is an incredible experience with a multitude of benefits for children. By trying to keep your children from adapting to the culture, learning the language, and spending time with the locals, you are limiting those benefits. Yes, absolutely teach them about their American roots. Celebrate American holidays and follow the news. But also give them permission to grow new roots in this new country. Yes, they will be different from their peers in America. They will have a unique perspective, a keen ability to adapt to new cultures, and an expanded worldview. They may even have challenges to work through because of their overseas upbringing, but attempting to keep them American while living overseas will not eliminate those challenges nor will it offer them the amazing benefits that can come with being a TCK.

CULTURAL HUMILITY

If you are living overseas, you likely made the move with some sort of goal in mind: humanitarian work, starting a business, working in the government, working as a missionary, teaching at a school, etc. While this is inherently good and is often the reason for moving overseas at all, these goals can make it easy to enter into the new culture, "guns blazing" ready to make changes. While I could get into all the negative implications this can have on the effectiveness of the work you do, the relationships you build with the locals, and the lack of long-term results you will likely see, I'd like to focus simply on what your attitude regarding entering a new culture teaches your children about relationship building.

Your children are watching you and are constantly learning from you. In your home culture, you know how to teach them the social norms, rules, customs, and values, but when you enter into a new culture, that set of rules changes and leaves you unsure of how to move forward. In a TED Talk with Julien Bourrelle, he lists three ways an individual can react when they move into a new culture: confront, complain, or conform.[49] When you choose, or subconsciously do any of these, you are subtly teaching your children how they, too, should navigate this new place and culture.

Confront: I could use the word "combat" interchangeably here. This is an attitude of fighting for things to be done "the right way." This attitude might come through in subtle ways such as mumbling, "If they would *just* do it this way, it would go so much faster!" or in deciding that, like the family in the podcast, your family will remain staunchly your passport nationality in every way possible while living in the different culture. This attitude can either be blatantly against cultural integration or just subtly unwilling to adapt. Either inherently teaches your children that the passport country's way is the best way and thus causes them also to be fighters against, instead of learners of, the new culture. It fosters a prideful attitude that says there is only "one right way" to do things and that the people in the new country clearly have it "wrong."

Complain: It drives us crazy when our children whine and complain, yet sometimes we subconsciously teach them that this is an appropriate attitude toward an unfavorable situation. I am as guilty of this as anyone. Living in a new culture can bring out annoyances and push your buttons, so to speak, on a daily basis. Your children are looking to you to learn the acceptable way of responding in those situations. Unfortunately, in my years in East Africa, I heard many parents complain to their children about the local people, customs, or ways of doing things. Often it was in the form of a nonchalant or joking comment, but then it would be repeated by the children. This does not foster an attitude of acceptance, humility, and respect, but instead enforces a "better than" mentality.

Conform: In other words, adapt. This does not necessarily mean that you need to change everything from your clothing to what your family values are, but it does mean learning to live like the people in the new culture do, at least in some ways. Adapting teaches your children that there is more than one right way to do things and encourages a love for diversity, a respect for all people, and a positive attitude in the midst of potentially frustrating and uncomfortable situations. As they see you working to adapt, accept, and learn the way that things are done in the new place, they, too, will feel the freedom to integrate into the new culture.

By living in a different culture, your children have the opportunity to become lovers of the world—global citizens—in an intimate, life-altering way that would not be nearly as possible if they lived only in their passport country. Don't squelch this opportunity by teaching them to confront or complain. As parents you are actively teaching your children what their attitude should be toward the new culture, so be vigilant about enforcing a positive attitude, one that encourages conformity and a positive, benefit-of-the-doubt response when something looks differently than what you, or they, are used to. Encourage and display the attitude of one who is a student of the culture, not a teacher there to convert the people to the "right" way of doing things.

DIVERSITY SALAD ACTIVITY

This activity is a fun way to get your family talking about the beauty of diversity. It can be a formally organized family activity, a simple conversation starter with your kids, or an addition to one of your family check-ins.

MATERIALS:

- A different piece of fruit for each person
- Large bowl
- Knife
- Cutting board
- Honey (optional)

ACTIVITY:

Sit around a table and hand each person a piece of fruit. Do not tell them what the activity is, and do not let them choose their fruit.

ASK:

- *How do you feel about the piece of fruit you were given?*
- *Is it very exciting to have only one kind of fruit?*
- *Do you wish you could share or trade your fruits?*

Have them hand the fruit back to you.

ASK:

- *How would these fruits all taste if they were together in a fruit salad?*

Cut up the fruit and put it in a large bowl. If desired, add a spoonful of honey. Give everyone a serving of fruit salad. As they eat it, talk about how good the fruit tastes when it is all mixed together.

ASK:

- *Which flavors do you think complement each other?*
- *Is the fruit salad better than if you would have just eaten the fruit you were given by itself?*
- *How is this like diversity?*

TELL THEM:

If everyone stayed only around the people who are just like them, that wouldn't be very exciting. People were made to be different—to look different, talk different, have different ideas and thoughts, and be better at different things! It is better when we mix together and learn from each other, just like the fruits are better mixed together. People who are different can complement each other because they have different strengths, ideas, and perspectives.

CULTURE LEARNING

As you learn to conform and adapt to a new culture, having a guide for how to do that practically can be helpful. Many businesses and organizations provide training for the adults that they send to live overseas. Some even offer children and teen programs to prepare the kids for the transition. Unfortunately, there is often a bit of a gap between the training the adults receive and the training the children receive. However, the family is moving into a new culture *together* and should therefore have tools that they can strategically use *together* as they learn a new language and culture. The children and the parents should not be operating with a different culture-learning skill set. Not only does that reduce the effectiveness of cultural integration, but more importantly, it lessens the opportunity for the family to experience the growth and connectedness that learning a new culture together can bring.

Here are five ways that you can integrate into your new culture as a family:

1. **Observe** *strategically.* Observation is one of the primary ways you can learn about a new culture. However, unless you do so strategically, you will miss a considerable amount of information. Because we get comfortable operating in our home society, we often participate without thinking. It is easy to allow ourselves to operate in this default mode when we enter a new culture instead of stepping back and taking the time to observe.

   Talk with your kids about observing with all of their five senses: touch, taste, smell, sight, and sound. Choose one sense per day to focus on. Perhaps have family member take turns deciding which sense to focus on each day. All throughout the day, talk about the things you all observe with that one sense. For example, all the things you smell throughout that day. You will be surprised by how much more you notice when you focus on only one sense at a time! Talk through your observations during your family check-in.

2. **Keep an observation journal.** As you explore with your five senses, keep a family journal of everything you observe. Take it everywhere with you and document every "sight," "touch," etc. each day. If your kids are old enough to write on their own, have them take turns documenting or give them each their own journal. During your family check-in at the end of the day, read through the documented observations.

3. **Ask questions.** The best way to learn about a new culture is by talking to the people who live there. Many families who move overseas enter into the expat community, and while this can be a great way to make friends, it is important to remember that you will never fully integrate into the culture by only spending time with other expatriates who live there, and that would be a huge loss for you and your children. Expatriates can only teach the culture of expatriates living in that country, but they will not be able to teach you about the true local culture. It can be intimidating for your children, and maybe you too, to talk with people from a different culture, so come up with a plan to make it less daunting.

    Have each family member come up with one open-ended question that they plan to ask multiple people on a particular day. For example, "What do you like best about your country?" or "Where do you buy your meat?" It can be as practical or as deep as you'd like, but the goal is to see how different people answer your question. Throughout the day, be looking for people to whom you and your kids can ask your questions. Are there common themes? During your nightly family check-ins, talk about this experience and the things that you learned.

4. **Make national family friends.** Again, it can be easy to get caught up in the "expat bubble," particularly if you relocated to the country for business. While it is not wrong and can be quite enriching to have expat friends, developing friendships with nationals is critical to learning

the culture. It is equally as important that your new group of national friends include "family friends." By that, I mean friends who have kids roughly the same age as yours and who are in a stage of life similar to yours. These are the friends to whom your family will be able eventually to ask the deeper questions about the values, expectations, and thought patterns of the culture. By spending time with these friends, asking questions, and observing how they interact with each other, their children, wait staff at a restaurant, etc., you will have the opportunity to shadow them and practice learning to act as a family from that culture.

5. **Go to the local hangouts.** Find out what the nationals do together with their families and do it! Do they go to the cinema? Are there local museums? Parks? Do they shop at the market as a family? Go to the beach? Bike around town? Instead of being tempted to check out all the tourist destinations, make it a point to spend your family free time the way that the nationals do. Not only will this teach you about the culture, but it is also a great way to make friends!

6. **Find a culture buddy.** A culture buddy is someone of any age, native to the culture where you are moving or living, who becomes a friend and is willing to teach your TCK the nuances and practicalities of the culture. I highly recommend that you find a culture buddy for each member of the family or find an entire local family who can be a culture buddy for your family.

The culture buddy is someone who will also, ideally, become a close friend. Have your TCK begin by meeting people when you arrive in the new country and scope out who they think might be a good fit for this role. The person should be close to your TCK's age and must have enough free time to spend being their culture buddy. Finding culture buddies for your children may happen organically if you are living in the local community and/or your TCKs are attending the local school. If you are not living in close proximity with the local people, it will be important to be more strategic about finding someone to teach the culture to your TCKs. You never know, perhaps one of those kids' parents will become *your* culture buddy!

What happens with the culture buddy depends most significantly on your TCKs' ages. A teenager, for example, would have very different goals than a six-year-old, but both would benefit greatly from the culture buddy concept.

1. For an older TCK, have them explain to their potential culture buddy what their hopes for the relationship are. For example, "I would love to be your friend, and I'm hoping that you would be willing to teach me about your culture. Perhaps we can spend time together a couple of days each week and you can teach me some things about life in this country?" This conversation isn't necessary for younger TCKs.

2. Once your TCK has found their culture buddy, have them set measurable goals that they would like to accomplish during their time together. Have only one goal per time spent together.

   If you have young TCKs, work with them to help them set their goals and keep them very simple. You may also consider setting a family goal that each family member works on separately with their culture buddy; then you can share and compare what you have learned with each other.

   Goals could include:
   - Learn how to greet others properly.
   - Learn how to play a common game.
   - Learn a song or chant that most everyone in the culture knows.
   - Learn three common nonverbal gestures and how to use them appropriately.
   - Learn to use the public transit system.
   - Learn how to navigate the food market like a local.
   - Do an activity that the locals would commonly do for fun (i.e., go to a movie, go to the beach, play a game, etc.).

3. Have your TCK explain their goal to their culture buddy and explain why learning that concept or skill is important to them.

For older TCKs and adults: Once you have developed a deeper relationship and have built trust with your culture buddy, you will be able to ask questions about the more complex nuances of the culture, such as why the people place value and importance on some things and not others. This is the stage when you really begin to understand the core of the culture.

The culture buddy is an easy concept that can be effectively used by a person of any age. It is a student-directed, strategic, relational method of learning the new culture that you are a part of. So, find a culture buddy for yourself and encourage your children and teens to do so as well!

LANGUAGE LEARNING

One of the most commonly talked about benefits of the TCK life is the chance for the children to learn new languages. This is not only beneficial to their development as children, but as our world gets increasingly smaller, the ability to speak more than one language will also give them an increased advantage in the workplace as adults—both because of their ability to speak a second language but also because of the broadened worldview it encourages.

If that's not enough, there are also incredible health benefits to language learning. According to the Canadian Council on Language Learning, learning another language as a child *eliminates* negative effects of aging on the brain and enhances the child's ability to focus and avoid distraction. Learning a second language has also been linked to increased skills in complex planning, creativity, and strategic problem solving.[50]

Here are some simple ways you can implement language learning as a family:

Label everything. One of my favorite ways to learn nouns is to label everything in the house. You can use sticky notes, index cards, fun paper, anything. It turns out that the most common nouns used are also typically the things you have around your house (door, floor, table, sink, bed, etc.). This is a great way to build your vocabulary. This was one of the very first things we did when we moved to Tanzania, and when I think of the word "door," I still picture the *mlango* note card that was taped to the back of our front door for years. This method is also great for visual learners who remember best by seeing the written word.

Listen, listen, listen. Children learn language first by hearing it. Babies listen for the first year or so before they begin to speak. It may not seem effective because you can't understand what is being said, but your child's brain (and yours too!) is actually beginning to unscramble and compartmentalize the sounds, and that will eventually lead to the understanding of words. The human brain is nothing short of amazing! Listen to the radio, to songs, to the local TV shows, to people speaking. Have the language in your house as much as possible.

Play games. This is a fun and easy way to work on language as a family. Below are some games you may already know that can be great for practicing a new language.

- **Uno**—This card game is great for learning the names of colors and numbers.
- **Card Games**—Make cards with a picture and corresponding word in the target language. You can either make these on the computer or cut paper squares and have your kids draw the pictures and write the words. You can use these cards to play:

  □ **Matching Game.** Put all the cards facedown. Each player flips two, trying to get a match (picture card and corresponding word card). If a match is found, the player gets another turn. Game continues until all matches have been found, and the player with the most matches wins.

  □ **Go Fish.** Play with the standard Go Fish rules trying to create matches with the correct words and pictures. Learn how to say, "Can I have?" or "Go fish" and "Yes" or "No," in the target language.

  □ **Speed.** Put all the picture cards faceup on the floor. Read the word cards while the players race to find the corresponding pictures. This is great for kids who are not reading yet.

- **Pictionary**—Use the cards you made for the above games to play Pictionary. Have one player draw a card (use the word cards if your kids are reading and the picture cards if they are not). The player draws the word/picture while the other players try to guess, using the target language, what they are drawing. To get the point, they have to guess the picture correctly in the target language. Keep score by giving each player a point when they guess correctly. If you have enough players, you can play this as a team game.

Sing songs. Songs are a great way to learn new vocabulary. I attended an international school during the first year we lived in Tanzania, and during each assembly we sang the Tanzanian national anthem. I learned a large variety of words by just learning that one song, and I loved feeling like I "fit in" because I could sing the national anthem! Search YouTube for children's songs in the target language, or find someone who speaks the language to teach you common songs. You can also get creative and make up your own songs for the phrases you are learning.

Websites and apps. My favorites are DinoLingo.com, Little Pim, and Gus on the Go. I had a five-year-old in one of my first trainings who was moving to Thailand. He didn't seem interested in language learning, but during free time I let him play on DinoLingo. About a week into the training, he was teaching the other kids words and phrases in Thai!

Provide learning opportunities, but don't pressure. Unlike adults, children, if given consistent exposure to the new language, will soak in the language without formal study. For this reason, pressuring them to learn is unnecessary and often counterproductive. Many children are intimidated by the idea of learning another language and may respond to this fear by being decidedly against the idea. If parents pressure their children in these situations, they are most likely going to resist learning, which not only hinders language acquisition but also creates a more difficult transition to life in the new place. Instead, use some of the above ideas to allow the new language to become an integrated part of your family life, and let your children learn at their own speed and in their own way. Before long they will surprise you with their new language abilities![51]

CULTURE AND EDUCATION

The question of schooling and education is often at the forefront of parents' minds as they prepare to live overseas. It can be challenging to drown out the multitude of strong opinions, and from what I have observed, there are many, many *strong* opinions. I often talk about this along with the topic of engaging in the culture because I believe the two are very interconnected. If you are thinking through the education aspect of TCK life, consider the following thoughts through the lens of culture learning.

TCK education consultant Barbara Tooley said to me in conversation about this topic, "It may seem obvious *why* you are sending your child to school, but it is not such a simple answer when you are living overseas." We tend to think of the purpose of school as purely academic education, but it is also for social, cultural, and language education. You may consider sending your TCKs to a local school for the sole purpose of culture and language learning. This is one of the best ways for children to integrate fully into the culture and allows them to develop an academic proficiency of the language (the highest level of fluency). If you choose this option, you will likely need to supplement at home with the education requirements of your passport country to ensure that they keep up to par with their grade level as well as maintaining academic language fluency in their first language. Older children who move overseas may need to focus more on academic requirements, so an international school, going to a boarding school, or homeschooling may be the best option. Cultural and language integration may then need to be done outside school.

It's also important to consider whom you want your children to befriend. Is your family seeking to integrate completely into the new country, so befriending the local neighbor kids is important? Or is your family seeking to be more involved in the existing expat community, so attending an international school and befriending other international students is a more appropriate goal? Because so much time is spent at school, that is likely where your TCKs will develop the closest friendships. Whom do you want those friends to be? How do you want their education to play into their culture-learning?

RELATED BENEFITS — A BROAD PERSPECTIVE:

TCKs are able to see that there is more than one "right" way of living life. They can appreciate doing things in a variety of different ways, and they don't assume that something is wrong just because it is unfamiliar to them. When they have integrated into different cultures, they learn that people have various ways of living life and that all of them can have positive elements. They are often quicker than the monocultural individual to assume that there is a good and valid reason for the way people are doing things as opposed to assuming they know a "better" way of doing it. This benefit becomes incredibly valuable when the TCK is in the workforce. In this era, it is common to work with a diverse team, global offices, clients from other countries, etc. It is often the TCKs who are able to build bridges between the different cultures and become valuable members of the business world.

THE MAIN IDEAS:

- Humbly engage in the culture by adapting instead of combatting or complaining.
- Give your children tools to learn the local language—not only does it give them great future opportunities, but it also has surprising health benefits!
- As you consider education options, look at them through the lens of cultural integration as well as the individualized needs of each of your children.

QUESTIONS TO CONSIDER:

- How do you talk about the culture and the local people where you are? What messages does that communicate to your TCKs?
- What steps can you take to increase your family's culture learning and language learning?
- Did anything surprise you about the conversation regarding education?

CHAPTER 9

Fostering Healthy Relationships

Healthy TCKs have learned to develop and maintain deep relationships that have spanned multiple seasons of their adult life.

TCKs are prone to many relationship hiccups, and like all of the common TCK challenges, relationship issues most often manifest in adulthood and thus may not be obvious to you yet if your children are still young. However, these practices and preventive tools can and should be applied throughout your TCKs' lives in the hope that their ability to develop healthy relationships as teens and adults is fostered and bred early on.

TCK relationship struggles have many elements that are important to be aware of.

BOREDOM

TCKs grow up in an incredibly transient community. Even if they are not the ones moving often, they are often affected by people constantly coming and going from their community. This keeps the friendships fresh. It is rare for TCKs to have friends whom they have lived in close proximity to for several years and even if they do, the community around them is often everchanging. Because of this, they are used to making friends, leaving or being left by those friends, and making a new set of friends. While they may (and should) grieve each of these losses, there is a pattern that begins to bring comfort. The pattern is that their mental alarm clock beeps after a certain amount of time in a relationship, signaling that they are bored and need fresh, new friends. Now, this is very rarely a conscious thought but instead a subconscious pattern that does not typically become destructive until adulthood. University is often the first time that TCKs live a four-year stint in one place with the same people, and it can bring to light this subconscious pattern.

In chapter 10 I talk more in depth about the TCK's "need for change," but how it impacts relationship is a topic in and of itself.

If you've noticed this in your TCKs, it's important to point out patterns that you see. I knew a TCK who would habitually change locations, friends, and romantic relationships each year. It was clear to me that there was a pattern, but she was not able to see and acknowledge it until it had gone on for several years and led to many burnt bridges. Though she was not receptive to me pointing out the pattern at first, the seed that I had planted began to become obvious to her as she continued to repeat this cycle. She eventually realized her need to learn how to develop long-term relationships and settle into a job and place for longer than a year. It was through having someone on the outside point out her pattern that she was eventually able to see it for herself and make positive changes.

FEAR OF ATTACHMENT BECAUSE OF LOSING FRIENDS FREQUENTLY

Like I talked about in chapter 4 regarding leaving well, frequent good-byes can be a source of relationship challenges for Third Culture Kids. After experiencing the repeated loss of friendships, it can be easy to decide to close off from potential new friends as a protective measure. This is one of the hardest challenges of the TCK life. There is no healthy way to make it easier to leave people you love, yet it would be a sad life never to build relationships for fear of leaving them.

For about a four-year period of my adult life, I avoided the pain of making friends that I would have to leave by not making friends at all. Though I was successful at leaving without any relationship-related grief, those were the loneliest years of my life, and it was more heartbreaking to realize that I was moving and there was no one to care or miss me. I decided that I was going to change that pattern in the next place, and though friends have come and gone, I have been incredibly grateful that I broke that cycle and learned to invest in friendships. I learned that I will always regret not building relationships more than I will regret moving away from people I love enough to miss.

When TCKs move often, it becomes easier to forgo deep friendships rather than deal with the hurt of frequent good-byes. Encourage your child to maintain friendships. TCKs become very skilled at *making* friends, but many have a more challenging time maintaining and developing *deep, lasting* friendships.

When TCKs have moved frequently, they may not want to invest deeply in friendships in order to avoid the pain of leaving friends yet again. The idea of deep friendships may also trigger that dreaded settled feeling. Teach your children to push past the fear and into those deep friendships. Encourage them to keep in touch with friends they have left behind *and* be willing to make new friends. Technology nowadays makes it much easier for TCKs to keep in touch with friends all over the world. Take advantage of it! Older TCKs may just need your gentle encouragement, while younger children may need more time and help on your part. It is worth the effort for your TCKs to have deep, lifelong friends who can love and support them in the midst of their moving, changing, and adapting.

PRIDE

Speaking about his years in university, Aneurin, author of TCK blog *Noggy Bloggy* said, "I grew incredibly bitter toward all of my friends at university who didn't understand me. These negative thought patterns usually led me to think lies about how narrow-minded and arrogant everyone was in the UK. As you can imagine, this didn't help me make friends, but pushed them away."[52]

His experience is not uncommon. In fact, this mentality stems from a commonly discussed issue of TCK pride. When TCKs have spent their whole lives being told how special they are, how diverse their worldviews are, and how different they are from kids their age back in their passport countries, it creates the perfect concoction for a prideful, "better-than" attitude. They go back to the countries their passports say they belong to, and suddenly they don't belong. When I experienced this for the first time in high school, this lack of belonging wasn't a surprise. In fact, I felt like I had been conditioned to know that I didn't *really* belong. I was unique and different, and in many respects, I liked it that way.

This attitude greatly hindered my ability to make friends. I remember thinking, "I'm so different from them, we could never be friends"; "I've seen so much of the world, and they've never left the state"; "I have so much life experience, and they've only just moved out of their parents' house"; "I'm a TCK; they could never understand me." I scroll through my Facebook feed and see people from that season whom I could have been great friends with had I only been willing to humble myself. I never outwardly treated them poorly, but my internal attitude said, "I'm better than you," and I regret the friendships that I missed out on because of that. I have learned in the years since then that there are, believe it or not, amazing people who have only ever lived in one country. As TCKs we are known for giving so much grace and respect to people outside our passport countries but extend so very little to the people in it. We would do ourselves good to combat that TCK arrogance and take a stance of humility. We may be surprised at the amazing people we befriend when we don't let our pride get in the way.

Here are some ways to think about combatting TCK pride:

Teach them how to get to know someone. Send your kid on a mission to get to know someone new. Have them learn five interesting facts about the new child at their school or in the community or perhaps someone who has been there for a while but doesn't seem to have many friends. What you are teaching them to do is not assume that they want or don't want to be friends with someone because of any preconceived notion. They will likely find that there is more to the person than they originally thought. Teach your children how to get to know people genuinely so that when they do return to their passport countries one day, they are already in the habit of taking the time to learn about someone before making any judgments.

Talk about *your* pride. Being vulnerable is tough, especially being vulnerable with your kids. But it is hard for children (and adults) to work through complex issues like pride without a good example. Talk about ways you have dealt with or are dealing with pride in a way that is at each of your children's maturity level. Kids love to hear stories of their parents' childhoods, so perhaps share a story of a time when you acted pridefully at their age. If you do something and realize that it was fueled by a prideful attitude, consider sharing that with your children. Vulnerability on your part will help your children to recognize what pride looks like, feel more comfortable about confessing that struggle to you, and learn to deal with it appropriately.

Teaching your children about pride may require you swallowing your own and humbling yourself enough to have these potentially difficult conversations. Pride has many faces and can leave so much wreckage in its wake, so knowing that this may be a particular challenge for TCKs, you are then equipped to give them tools to combat that attitude and practice humility.

TECHNOLOGY

Technology has enhanced the ability for this generation of TCKs to maintain long-term relationships with others no matter where in the world they are. This can be both a huge asset and also a potential pitfall. Third Culture Kids live a mobile lifestyle in a world where others around them are also constantly coming and going. This continuous exchange of people makes it difficult for TCKs to develop deep friendships both logistically (because either they or their new friend may leave before the relationship deepens) and emotionally (they begin to fear attempting a deep relationship because there is a high chance that they or their friend will leave).

The use of social media seems to be a good solution to this problem.

TCKs can make friends and, even when they or their friend leaves, keep up with them on Facebook, Instagram, Snapchat, or a plethora of other social media platforms. This, in some ways, eliminates the reasons TCKs find not to pursue friendships because a long-distance friendship is now easy. However, it also *increases* the common TCK problem of forgoing deep friendships.

Social media becomes a great way for TCKs to have a thousand surface-level friendships with people all across the globe without the risk of being emotionally hurt by someone leaving yet again.

To the TCK who has been hurt, this may sound like a great option. They may even do this subconsciously. TCKs are notoriously great at the beginning stages of relationships. Thus, they are prone to making friends easily, "friending" them on Facebook, and never allowing those friendships to become real, deep relationships. Social media makes friendship safe for TCKs because they don't have to go deep in order to be "friends" and to keep up with each other's lives from the other side of the globe. Social media *can* be a huge asset to twenty-first-century TCKs, but it is so important that it doesn't also become a tool for keeping friendships at a safe, surface level. This does not mean that TCKs need to be, or should be, "deep" friends with everyone or that they need to have a significant number of deep friendships, but it *is* critical to their well-being that they have at least a handful of people who truly know and love them.

If you are raising TCKs, encourage them to be intentional about developing deep friendships with people locally. Once they have those deep friendships, those relationships can be fostered and continued on through the use of social media if they or their friend moves away. Because it can be easy (and often feels safer) for TCKs to spend their time on social media with acquaintances and simply add more people to their "friends" list, instead of working to develop deep friendships, it is critical that, as parents, you actively encourage them to step out of their comfort zone and let people really get to know them. While there is always a risk of your child or your child's friend moving away, there is a bigger risk to never developing real, deep friendships. Thankfully, social media is available to allow those friendships to continue even if one day they have to be long-distance.

TOO MANY FRIENDS

According to anthropologist Robin Dunbar, human brains have a limit on how many meaningful relationships they can keep track of. The broadest category is "casual friends" and we typically have room for about 150; the next level is about fifty close friends; next is the intimate group of fifteen friends; and finally, the core group of five is often, but not always, family members.[53]

Third Culture Kids face this challenge when it comes to friendships. They easily exceed Dunbar's numbers, and this can be tricky for them to manage. When I work with college-age TCKs, they are often experiencing this challenge for the first time. They have many friends back in their host countries, others who have moved to other parts of the world, and now new friends in college. I have found an interesting pattern during these sessions. Either they have too many people they are trying to fit into their core and intimate friend groups, or they have very few in those groups. It is rarely an even spread, which Dunbar found is natural for monocultural individuals. When I address this with TCKs, we talk about two things:

1. **The reality that it is okay for friends to move through the categories.** It is often a relief that they don't have to maintain so many friendships in order for those friends to stay in their core and intimate groups. It is not only acceptable but necessary for TCKs to allow for friends to move fluidly throughout the groups depending on their season of life and their location.

2. **The TCK's tendency to close off from core and intimate relationships as a defense mechanism.** This may be because they are too overwhelmed by the reality of people moving in and out of those groups. In these situations, I stress to TCKs the importance of allowing themselves to develop deep relationships. Without people in those "core" and "close" groups, TCKs are prone to loneliness and isolation.

A great exercise for older TCKs is to have them list their five "core" relationships and fifteen "close" relationships. Then ask the following questions:

- How often do people move in and out of the core and close groups?
- Do you have too many or too few people in each category?
- Are the majority other TCKs?
- Do you find it hard to label friends as "close"?

You can download a worksheet for this at TCKTraining.com/worksheets.

These questions do not have right or wrong answers but can simply bring awareness to any patterns that your TCK might have regarding relationships. It is important for them to begin thinking through these patterns as they typically only intensify as TCKs age. If you can help them to recognize patterns early on, it is easier for them to notice and adjust their tendencies in the future.

RELATED BENEFITS – NONDISCRIMINATORY FRIENDS:

Third Culture Kids are marvelous at building relationships and making people feel comfortable—particularly those who are in minority groups. They easily befriend those who may be outsiders because they have likely felt that way as well. This is a great skill and explains the TCK's often very diverse friend group. They tend to be less segregated and judgmental than monocultural individuals, and this is certainly a trait to be praised!

THE MAIN IDEAS:

- Relationship building is difficult for most TCKs and only gets harder if not addressed and prevented.
- Because of the transient nature of the expat community, TCKs are often unfamiliar with long-term friendships. When they grow into adults and have the opportunity to engage in long-term friendships, they often get bored or insecure and end the relationship. This can develop into a pattern.
- TCKs have a difficult time developing friendships in their passport countries. Some of this is due to arrogance and some is due to a lack of fitting in.
- Technology can be helpful in allowing TCKs to maintain long-term relationships, but it can also prevent them from engaging in deep, meaningful relationships and thus should be carefully used.
- TCKs tend to have either too many or not enough friends in their "core" and "close" friend groups. They need to take stock of their friends and either allow themselves to let friends move more fluidly in and out of their circles or be more intentional about developing more "core" and "close" friends.

QUESTIONS TO CONSIDER:

- Have you noticed any patterns in your TCKs' relationships?
- What do your own relationships look like, and what does that model for your TCKs?
- What conversations can you have with your TCKs to address any relationship challenges they may be facing?

CHAPTER 10

Wrestling with Restlessness

Healthy TCKs have learned how to control the need for change instead of letting it control them, know how to combat their restlessness in healthy ways, and allow themselves to be "settled" in the necessary areas of life.

"The Travel Itch" by Gwen Thomas

I call myself a wanderer, an adventurer,
but that's just a blanket I hide under
to hide from the reality of my life.
Truth be told, I am a runner.
And I don't mean the type that puts on shoes,
and jogs around town a few times.
I mean I am the type who abandons,
and as harsh as it sounds a coward.
It comes every few years,
as I start to get settled into a place,
I feel the itch,
deep in my mind and in my body.
It's the feeling of suffocation,

a tightness in my chest.
I try inhaling deeply,
reminding myself of all the good things,
all the homely things I have set around me.
But it just makes it worse.
I am ready to run again,
to pick up and leave on an adventure.
Maybe I'll come back,
maybe I won't.
Either way, wind in my hair,
and past behind me,
it will feel good.
At least for a bit,
while reality is kept at bay.
But eventually loneliness knocks at the door.
Somehow, he always finds me,
no matter how sneaky I am.
Each time he shows up with
the name "deserter" on his tongue.
I know I hurt others.
I don't want to.
But somehow, staying is too painful.
I know I desire intimacy and depth.
I want to know someone so well
that I couldn't imagine leaving them behind.
I want a love that runs deep,
but I never expect that for anyone.
Restlessness runs deep in my veins,
and it comes roaring like a lion,

when routines are set and life is calm.
It's insistent on noise and change,
because the quiet invites vulnerability,
and the lion inside is terrified of that silent child.
It bares its teeth,
shakes its mane,
and prepares for a fight.
Nothing is more terrifying than being trapped.
And so I wander.
I find a new rhythm,
walk strange streets,
and see faces unfamiliar.
I sleep in beds not my own,
I search for superficial love and friendship,
so they will accept me,
but not too much.
Because once I get attached,
I will want to run again.
I don't want this though.
I want to meet someone who tames the fear
and coaxes the child out.
Who can be constant but never constraining,
like the ocean waves.
Always coming back to the shore,
but still wild and free.
I could love someone like that.
Someone who knows the pulse of restlessness in their veins,
and is ready to be home for me on every adventure.

Every so often I get to work with college-age TCKs. The poem above, quoted in its entirety with permission from the author, was written by one of these students. I love working with this age group because they are in the midst of truly navigating the interplay of being a TCK and growing into an adult. Recently, I led a group discussion with about twenty of these TCKs at a local university. Prior to the day of the discussion, I had the leader send out a list of optional topics for them to vote on. The topic "Need for Change" won by a landslide. I wasn't surprised, because I think this is one of the TCK challenges that is most surprising to young adult TCKs and often goes unnoticed until someone points it out.

To begin the discussion, I asked, "Since starting university have you, by your own choice . . ."

- dropped classes?
- changed majors?
- changed jobs?
- changed schools?
- changed friends/friend groups?
- had several romantic relationships or one that went very deep and then ended abruptly?
- moved houses/dorms?
- changed churches?

For each question more than half the group raised their hands.

I then asked, "What process did you go through to make that decision?"

Their answers were:

- "I just did it without any thought."
- "Over time I emotionally pulled away from the people/place until it was just natural and easy to leave."
- "I found reasons why I disliked teachers, friends, classes, my girlfriend, so then it gave me a reason to leave that wasn't my problem."
- "There wasn't a process. I actually didn't realize there was a pattern there until just now, but I could answer 'yes' to almost all of those. I guess it just felt so natural that I never thought anything of it."

We spent the next two hours talking about this need for change, how to be aware of its role in their lives, and how to combat it in healthy ways. We will do the same in this chapter.

THE NEED FOR CHANGE

Third Culture Kids (TCKs) have an exceptional ability to become cultural chameleons. They can subconsciously pick out the subtleties in a new culture and operate successfully in that culture even if they only move between their passport country and one host country. Because of this, adapting becomes their lifestyle. More than that, I believe that adapting becomes their comfort zone.

The funny thing is that TCKs often don't realize this. Many dream of a settled life in a small town, where their children can grow up in the same house, go to the same school, and have the same people in their lives who knew them from birth. For a long time, this was my dream. This sounded comfortable. However, each time I got close to this settled feeling, I would get *uncomfortable,* and the clock in my head would go off that said, "Time for a new place, new things, new people!" and I would once again be on the move.

Still, I thought it was a settled feeling that I was searching for.

After many conversations with TCKs and colleagues who also work with the TCK community, I found that I was not alone in this. For the majority of monocultural individuals, being *settled* and *adapted* is comfortable. You have "arrived" when you have a stable job, purchase a house, and start to build a life. Moving is considered one of the top five most stressful life events.[54] However, for the majority of TCKs, moving is thrilling, exciting, and *comfortable*. This process of *settling* and *adapting* to a new environment is familiar territory, and they know how to navigate it well. It is when they begin to settle for good that they feel uncomfortable and must make the conscious decision to wade into the uncharted territory of being *settled* and *adapted*.

WHAT'S THE ISSUE?

The majority of TCKs will always have the itch for change, and because of their upbringing, the "easy" solution to a difficulty is often a big change. Of Third Culture Kids interviewed, 54 percent fly at least four times per year and live in an average of four different countries in their lifetime, so cross continental flights and relocations are not daunting for most TCKs.[55] This is where TCKs differ from monocultural individuals who feel they have a need for change. When a monocultural individual feels they need a change in their life, they might redecorate their house. When a TCK feels they need a change, they might move to Iceland.

The TCK's solution to their mental alarm clock is often a move (sometimes cross-culturally), a major career change, a school change, or a relationship change. These may not seem problematic and, on the surface, often aren't when the TCK is a child, teen, or young adult. However, when they don't learn how to satisfy this need in a healthy way, and this "need" arises later in adulthood, it can be incredibly crippling to their career, marriage, family life, and more.

Despite the clear challenges, the adaptable and flexible nature of your children can be a great quality. It is a skill they have learned (or will learn) out of necessity, in order to cope with the transition between cultures. And it will serve them very well in life if they learn to use it effectively. Fortunately, you as parents can help your TCKs navigate this change and develop the awareness needed to make this trait healthy and productive.

COMBATTING THE RESTLESSNESS

Talk with your TCKs about this concept of being comfortable in the adapting process and less comfortable in a settled life. Your children may not understand, and your teenagers may not want to hear it, but we can hope that when they become adults and are faced with this challenge, they will remember your words and be proactive about controlling the change instead of letting it control them.

If you know that your TCKs will likely struggle with the need for change into and through adulthood, then you can subtly teach them, from a young age, how to channel that need appropriately. Talk about the things that you can routinely and flippantly change (house decor, wardrobe, bedrooms, hairstyles, etc.) and the things that you really need to think about before you change (friends, places, schools, jobs, etc.). Help your child embrace their love, and even need, for positive change.

Leave well. Remember RAFT from chapter 4? When you leave your passport country for the first time, and during every "leave" after that, make sure you are intentional about applying the RAFT concept. It is nearly impossible to settle well in a new place if you have not left the previous place well.

When we know that we are about to leave people for an extended period of time, we tend to disconnect emotionally from people prematurely. This can very easily become a habit for TCKs and can lead to a lot of "burned bridges" and unresolved grief over the years. Your children need to learn how to leave well from a young age.

Show your children how to settle. It can be tempting, especially as an adult, to live with one foot in this new culture and leave the rest of yourself back in your passport culture. Some people do this by trying to keep their home and family life as "American" (or whatever your original nationality is) as possible while living in a different country. This will not do your TCKs any good and will definitely not teach them how to settle well. Wherever you are living, dive in. Make friends. Learn the language. Eat the food. Engage.

Because TCKs become incredibly good at adapting and integrating, this lifestyle will become their comfort zone. That is okay as long as they also learn to step outside their comfort zone and to settle in some areas of life.

Teach the process of making a healthy change. Be an example of the *process* of making big changes. If you are looking at moving or changing your child's school, talk with them about it, make a pros-and-cons list, make it a big decision. Often parents of TCKs don't invite their children into the decision-making process and instead only tell them once a decision has been made. In some scenarios this is necessary, but in most, allowing them to be a part of the process gives them the opportunity to see changes made well.

I want to be clear that the healthy version of a TCK who has overcome the need for constant adapting is not *necessarily* the TCK that settles down in one place for the rest of his or her life. That may be the case, but most likely it is not.

The healthy TCK realizes that they have a need for change and knows that they are more comfortable with the adapting process than with the settled life. However, they have learned how to control the need for change instead of letting it control them. They are willing to be somewhat uncomfortable so that they can live a settled life in the areas necessary to maintain personal and family health. For TCKs, doing this effectively is a lifelong learning process.

ON BEING SENTIMENTAL—OR NOT

For me, learning to settle in a healthy way continues to be a process. I have begun to put down some roots, yet anytime something threatens to drive the roots further into the ground faster than I'm ready for, my restlessness strikes again.

My grandmother passed away just before Christmas two years ago. Though we lived most years on different continents, she was the most present grandmother during my childhood—especially before we moved to Africa. During those years, she was the one to pick me up from school when I was sick, she came to every performance (including backyard musical productions), and she loved to take me shopping.

She was a very sentimental lady who saved everything that I made her, collected anything that might one day be valuable, and made sure that her home was furnished with the finest things.

After her passing, my parents flew to her home in Florida to clean out the house and drive the things of sentimental value back to Oregon in a U-Haul. She had left me some antique furniture and several boxes of other items that were special to her and that I'm sure she hoped would be special to me one day too.

As I added some of her furniture to my home and started to pull things out of boxes, I had an uneasy, anxious feeling that I couldn't shake. As I began to process through it, I realized that it was the permanence of it that was bothering me.

For the first time in my life, I have stuff in my house that I can't just get rid of.

Up until this point, all of our furniture, and pretty much everything other than what could comfortably fit into a few suitcases, were all things that I didn't have any personal attachment to. A better way to say it: "I could sell everything in my house tomorrow, move across the world, and not be sad about leaving the 'stuff.'"

Not having sentimental things gave me a sense of freedom. We could pick up and move if we wanted to and could fit everything sentimental in a few fifty-pound bags. I like that.

But inheriting these large pieces of furniture that I hope to pass down to my own girls one day yet which don't fit in a suitcase has made my TCK self incredibly uneasy. Being sentimental ties me down and goes against my adventurous, minimalist, flexible, pick-up-and-go nature.

This has been a recent reminder that I am still learning to settle and to be content rooting myself for a while. I'm still learning to invest in friendships and to plant trees—both of which need time settled in one place to grow. And I'm learning to appreciate a house that now contains pieces of my history and furniture that still smells a bit like my grandmother.

Marilyn Gardner's book *Between Worlds* has be instrumental in helping me to process the angst of being rooted. She says, "But perhaps being rooted gives strength. Perhaps being rooted doesn't give up who I am; perhaps it means that I securely use my past as a bridge to my present."[56] I am learning the strength that comes from being rooted and allowing these settled elements of my life to be a beautiful part of my present, recognizing that they don't take away from my past.

As your TCKs wrestle with the ideas or realities of becoming more settled and rooted, encourage them with this: it is not a threat to who they are as a TCK, but instead is a strength that, when learned intentionally, will enable them to weave a beautiful life of being flexible and adaptable yet wonderfully rooted. When we let ourselves grow roots, we allow places, people and memories of them to be a significant part of our story. With this perspective in mind, the inheritance of my grandmother's furniture no longer becomes a symbol of my stuck-ness but points to the rootedness I had during the seasons that she was an integral part of my life.

DIFFICULTY PLANNING AHEAD

Because of TCKs' adaptable nature, they often struggle to plan ahead. They take life as it comes, and many don't feel a need to control it, but instead feel free to embrace and enjoy it. This likely stems from the fact that they grew up with a lifestyle that taught them that if they don't climb that mountain today, they may not be around to do it tomorrow or the friends they want to climb it with may not be. They jump on opportunities to spend time with people, to see the sights, and to go on adventures. For some, this can continue on in a healthy way that allows for a spontaneous yet responsible lifestyle. For others, however, it can become a hurdle in adult life. If they are constantly looking for the next exciting thing to do and aren't thinking about how anything fits into a larger time frame than the next twenty-four hours, it can lead to irresponsibility that affects their marriages, parenting, ability to hold a job, etc.

Help your TCKs learn to plan ahead by doing so as a family. While this may be difficult in some ways because of your own transient lifestyle, look for opportunities in which you can plan ahead and openly share the process with your TCKs. It may look like thinking through university requirements while still in primary school or planning for the next vacation six months in advance. The key is to engage your TCKs in the planning process so that, while they may still have difficulty planning ahead in their adult lives, they have at least experienced an example of the planning process that they can look back on.

RELATED BENEFITS — ADAPTABILITY:

While the restlessness that TCKs experience can be a challenge, it yields a unique ability to adapt that makes TCKs excellent at fitting into new situations, with new people, in new cultures. Psychologist Guy Winch says, "Our ability to have life satisfaction, to be happy [and] to have good relationships really depends on our ability to adapt."[57] TCKs have that ability in strides thanks to their upbringing. This ability is not only helpful for daily life but is also an increasingly valuable skill in the workplace. TCKs often find that they are praised by their employers as adults and their flexibility and adaptability are usually a primary feature.

THE MAIN IDEAS:

- Because of the fluid nature of the TCK life, TCKs often develop a need for change that makes it difficult for them to settle and adapt in many areas of life.
- It is critical that they are taught from a young age how to manage this need for change in a healthy way so that they can control it instead of letting it control them.
- When the need for change is combatted in a healthy way, their amazing ability to adapt can be used in productive and positive ways.

QUESTIONS TO CONSIDER:

- In what ways can you be more intentional about helping your TCKs learn to manage their need for change?
- Have you noticed these challenges in your TCK yet? If not, why is it still important to address them now?
- How can you begin helping them to develop the skill of planning ahead?

CHAPTER 11

Recognizing TCK Shame

Healthy TCKs are able to be vulnerable by lifting their mask and showing who they uniquely are, not the perfect version for the culture they are surrounded by and recognize that this is not a shameful act but, on the contrary, is incredibly brave.

TCKs cannot fully grow as individuals or contribute to society if they are living their lives behind a mask. As shame researcher Dr. Brené Brown says, "It takes incredible courage and vulnerability to take off your mask."[58] For many TCKs, what is under the mask feels shameful. Under the mask is a self that is unsure of who they are, where they fit, how to act, and what the "correct" thing to do or say is in any given situation outside their TCK community—most especially in their passport country. TCKs grow up perfecting their "masks" more, I believe, than anyone else. It is a survival skill, critical to their well-being while living in any society. One serious issue for TCKs is feeling that they are never able to take off the mask—especially when living outside a TCK community as many do in adulthood. Taking off the mask often means the shameful admission that they don't actually know what they are doing, and for a TCK who has been incredibly successful at masking that reality for decades, the whole idea seems counterintuitive and terrifying.

TAKING OFF MY MASK

It has only been in recent years that I have truly braved lifting my mask. For me this has looked like a willingness to ask questions that clearly reveal that I'm not quite as "in tune" with the culture as I let on. At the risk of sounding trivial, here is a recent example. I have lived back in my passport country, the United States, since coming here for university ten years ago. For the past ten years, I have played "style" very safe in fear of making a cultural faux pas. I've worn very neutral colors, never any bold makeup, and a very modest and unassuming hairdo. Taking off my mask has meant recently asking close friends to help me shop for stylish clothes, choose lipstick colors, and experiment with styling my hair differently. My questions have been, "What does a mom, who also works a professional job, wear in the culture of this country, state, and city in order to look put together? What does professional attire look like? What do I wear when I take my children to the park? How do I dress for my age group and stage of life? *Where* do I shop?" Being willing to admit to my friends that I am unsure of these things has not only helped me to branch out and feel more confident in my different roles, but it has eradicated the shame I felt for so long as I hid the fact, even to my closest friends, that I didn't intuitively know these things like everyone else seemed to.

CHAMELEONS AND SHAME

Sometimes the TCK mask expands to the whole self and, like a chameleon, the TCK stealthily blends into their environment. They have a wonderfully complex ability to morph into the present culture, environment, and situation, and to blend in a way that makes them look like a native, though they are often anything but.

This trait is a valuable form of protection. It keeps them from always looking like the outsider (though it may not keep them from constantly feeling like one), and it helps them to be successful and accepted in any culture.

I have noticed in my work with TCKs that it is typically between the ages of thirteen and twenty-five that they take on the most chameleon-like form. In this time period, they are uncomfortably aware of the peering eyes of those around them (real or perceived), and they are simultaneously not yet comfortable in their own skin—or they don't even know what their own skin looks like because it has changed colors so often.

While this adaptability can be helpful, I have realized in my own life that the reason behind it, especially during those years, went far deeper than just wanting to fit in.

I was a chameleon because I knew that to be exposed, to change to the wrong color at the wrong time, to forget momentarily (or genuinely not know) how to go about life like a competent young adult in my passport culture would be incredibly shameful.

The underlying reason for mastering the trait of adaptability was shame.

For many teenage and young adult TCKs, this shame dictates their lives. They put an incredible amount of energy and emotion into looking like they belong—out of fear that they will be found out. Out of fear that they will misstep and someone will see it and shame them, verbally or mentally, for their cultural faux pas. Out of fear that people will silently applaud the inner voice telling them they truly will never fit in.

Shame is not often talked about in the TCK world, though I believe it is a significant issue for this growing population.

Unfortunately, shame is a parasite in relationships. It keeps us from true, deep connection. When we put on any sort of mask in our relationships, there is only a certain depth to which we can go with people before it begins to feel like they are too close to being able to see underneath our mask. We can't let that happen, so to avoid it, we distance ourselves, pretend to be "close" to people, or cut off relationships that begin to feel too exposing. This TCK shame, while it may seem like a small issue, can have catastrophic results when it manifests as a lack of willingness to engage in deep relationships and ultimately leads to isolation.

If you are a parent of a TCK or are working with TCKs, consider bringing the word "shame" into your vocabulary. Spend a significant amount of time helping your TCKs to wrestle through the things that are core to who they are. How do those core traits play out in their lives? What do they do because it is a part of who they are, and what do they do out of fear of not blending in with everyone else?

I am letting out a TCK secret by writing this chapter. Without exposing this issue of shame, many would never be aware of the deep well that is this issue because we are so excellent at hiding it. Now that you are aware, I pray that you take the issue seriously, begin to notice when something that you see in your TCKs is rooted in shame, and lovingly bring it into the light.

It is important for TCKs to befriend older TCKs who have learned to live authentically. They desperately need the example of someone who knows how to chameleon well but chooses not to for the sake of healthy relationships—especially in the passport country. This person may be a counselor who is also a TCK, a TCK mentor at university, or someone whom they connect with through a TCK Facebook group. The challenge with this is that it needs to happen incredibly intentionally because it won't likely happen naturally.

A NOTE TO YOUNG ADULT TCKS

As someone who is often in this mentor role for college-age TCKs, I wrote a letter from that perspective. If you have young adult TCKs of your own or support TCKs in that age group, feel free to pass this on. You can download a printout at TCKTraining.com/worksheets.

Dear young adult TCK,

You are an excellent adapter. But you know this. You have been praised for this skill your entire life. You are great at adjusting and adapting, and you have probably found your chameleon nature to be a valuable and necessary trait. It is one of your many superpowers. But what is the reason behind this constant adapting? I know for me the reason was shame.

When your adapting is fueled by shame, your primary motivation changes from learning how to live in the culture to constantly hiding any trace that you don't already know how to live in the culture.

Unfortunately, this shame has consequences.

If your goal is to look like you fit in, to look like you know what to do, to look like you are confidently and competently navigating the culture, then you are simply striving to portray and uphold an image. Not only is this exhausting, but it often prevents true connection and support.

In my college years, I would have thought, "If I reach out for support, I am admitting to myself that I am not as good of a chameleon as I thought I was."

Not only is that uncomfortable, it is shameful—especially for a TCK who is praised throughout their life for enviable adaptability.

But, dear TCK, the price to pay for looking like we have it all together is the love and support of someone who knows that we really don't.

We need people to whom we can ask silly questions about how the post office works, how to use the self-checkout at the grocery store, and how to use (or if you even *should* use!) the public transit system. Someone who lets us hang up our chameleon suit in exchange for a homemade dinner and great, nonthreatening conversation about our many global adventures.

One of the greatest gifts for a TCK is finding people with whom they don't need to put on a flawless show of brilliant adaptability.

But I don't think the challenge is necessarily finding these people. **The challenge is overcoming the shame that says that reaching out to them is weakness.**

So, I challenge you. Consider the reason behind your ever-adapting nature. Then, humbly take steps to find your people—the people who will get to know the you underneath your adapting self.

I know it's hard, but you can do it. After all, we TCKs are always up for a good challenge.

Unmasked,
Lauren

As your TCKs mature, I pray that they begin to discover their unique colors—the colors that don't change out of fear of being found out, but instead the colors that they are proud to be wherever they are.

RELATED BENEFITS — HEALTHY SELF-CONFIDENCE:

Because of their diverse background, your TCKs' identities may not look exactly like any one place or people, but they are instead beautiful and healthy mixtures of all the cultures that have made them who they are. Once they learn that they can take off their masks and be okay with not displaying the perfect versions of themselves for the culture they are in, they can show their beautiful kaleidoscope of colors. They can be confident and proud of who they are and all they have been shaped by.

THE MAIN IDEAS:

- TCKs who struggle in adulthood often don't reach out for help because it feels shameful.
- It is important to talk about shame and the TCK's chameleon nature that keeps TCKs from showing their true selves.
- It is in young adulthood that this shame typically intensifies, so it is important for TCKs to be aware of that and to combat it consciously.

QUESTIONS TO CONSIDER:

- Is "shame" in your family's vocabulary? Consider how you might have a conversation about it with your TCKs.
- In what ways do you see your TCKs changing depending on the culture?
- Are they adapting in ways that are potentially unhealthy?

CHAPTER 12

Managing Subconscious Expectations

Healthy TCKs are aware of their subconscious expectations of life and of themselves and have learned to offer themselves grace for their imperfections and develop contentment in their lifestyle.

Third Culture Kids have spent their lives hopping on international flights, traveling to exotic destinations, and interacting with different cultures and people around the world. For most, the globally mobile lifestyle is no longer a given once they reach adulthood. Flights are no longer paid for by a parent's organization or business, and they realize that working a job is a necessary part of life and that having a job makes traveling the world challenging. Many assume they will just naturally settle down into this new rhythm, but when they get to the point of actually doing so, they realize it feels far from natural. They may not realize that their subconscious expectations of how life is "supposed to go" contributes to their sense of restlessness, rootlessness, and general unhappiness with how life is unfolding. Many times TCKs don't realize that they even desire to live the same lifestyle that they did growing up until they attempt to settle down and find they have a constant itch for change, as I discussed in chapter 10.

The TCK's overseas upbringing created the belief that if they are not living a globally mobile lifestyle, they are settling for something lesser. Something boring and mundane and *normal.* Unfortunately, overseas living as adults may not be a feasible, or at least simple, option. Or perhaps they genuinely do not desire to live overseas again but still cannot seem to find fulfillment in a stable lifestyle.

Josh Sandoz, a counselor who works with adult Third Culture Kids in Seattle, said to me,

"Subconscious, unmet expectations are one of the root causes of many of the issues that I see adult TCKs dealing with."

People who grow up in a single country typically expect that they will live a similar lifestyle as the people around them. They see their grandparents, parents, their peers, and others following similar paths. For example, complete high school, go to college, start a career, get married, have children, retire. Their culture has displayed what the natural life trajectory looks like, and if an individual decides to do something outside the norm, it is usually a conscious, positive decision or an act of rebellion. TCKs, however, grow up living a lifestyle that may not be possible to maintain after they leave their parents' household. They leave for college, realize over time that they are feeling restless living in one place, and simultaneously know that they can't simply return to the lifestyle with which they are comfortable and familiar.

Because many adult TCKs don't realize that subconscious expectations may be the root cause of their discontentment, the issue can go unresolved for many years. They often end up in the office of a counselor with depression, anxiety, relationship issues, or many of the other challenges that we have discussed.

As TCKs work to think through their hopes, desires, and ideals for adulthood, they must first acknowledge and deliberately discover what the expectations are that their childhood overseas lifestyle instilled. Then they can begin to decide which aspects they want to integrate into their adult lives and which they want to leave behind as they forge their own path.

ADDRESSING EXPECTATIONS

How do you talk about your overseas life with your TCKs? Do you imply that it is the best way to live? Think about the messages that you send to your TCKs as you talk about living overseas versus living in your passport country.

It is important to have conversations that allow these subconscious expectations to surface. Emphasize that while your family is living overseas and is enjoying many aspects of that lifestyle, that does not mean that it is "better than" any other. As you well know, there are absolutely challenges that come with the overseas life as well. Your goal with these conversations is to simply level out the expectations by talking about the pros and cons of different ways of life. Perhaps say things like, "What are some of your favorite parts about living overseas?" "What are some hard things about living here?" "What would it be like if we lived back in our passport country and had never lived overseas?" "What would be some good things about that?" "What things might be hard?"

Talking about the positives *and* negatives of different lifestyles helps your TCKs not to settle into a belief that by living one lifestyle and not another, they are missing out. Instead, they are simply trading one list of pros and cons for another. Many adult TCKs, after realizing that they are unsatisfied with how their lives are playing out, think, "If I just moved there, everything would be better." But then they move there and realize that there are still challenges. Or they realize that they do not have the ability to move "there" and resign themselves to the idea that they will never be happy. Subconscious expectations about the "ideal" lifestyle will ultimately zap the joy out of any lifestyle. TCKs stuck in that rut will always be searching for the "better than" way of life that they felt they had growing up and will ultimately find that they cannot recreate it exactly how it was. They have to create their own and accept (and expect!) that there truly are both positives and negatives to any.

GROWING UP

It is also important to talk with your TCKs about what life might look like for them when they grow up. What are they interested in pursuing as a career? Does that career lend itself to living overseas again? If not, is that truly a door they want to close? Will they want to live in one place long-term? What will happen when their mental alarm clock goes off after three years in the same place and they have the itch to move and start over? What happens if they marry someone who never wants to move? Children and teenagers can be fickle and shortsighted, and that will likely affect their answers to these questions. That is okay! Your goal is not to help them create the perfect trajectories for their lives through these conversations but simply to get them thinking about how career choices, college choices, relationship choices, etc. will have a direct impact on the lifestyles they end up living. These conversations are meant to bring these subconscious expectations out of hiding so that they are easier for your TCKs (and you) to identify when they start to creep up in adulthood.

If they have thought through these questions at different points throughout their lives, it will be less of a shock and less of an identity crisis when they have to answer them in adulthood.

TCKs are often told their whole lives how lucky, blessed, unique they are because of their global upbringing. They are constantly reminded of the incredible opportunity that they have to live in different places around the world and not be "normal" like someone who has been raised in only one country. While overseas living is absolutely a unique and wonderful experience for TCKs, what happens when they grow up and are expected (either by themselves, by parents, or by society) to settle flawlessly into a life lived in a single country? Or when they try to recreate their overseas upbringing and find that it is not what they had expected and not even possible?

Subconscious expectations, because they often go unnoticed, can wreak havoc on the life of an adult TCK. It is, therefore, important to bring these expectations into the light so they can be considered and managed well. This can only happen through healthy relationships. As you raise up your TCKs or work with TCKs, having a deep enough relationship to have deep conversations about lifestyle expectations will be hugely beneficial. Then they are better able to connect the dots mentally when they, one day as adults, realize that they really do have expectations about how their lives "should" go. It is incredibly freeing for many adult TCKs to realize that there isn't one perfect lifestyle that they have to find in order to live a fulfilled life. Instead, they learn that any lifestyle has both its benefits and challenges and that their lives just might end up looking differently than what they had subconsciously expected.

EXPECTATIONS OF SUCCESS

Winston Churchill says, "Success is not final, failure is not fatal: it is the courage to continue that counts." TCKs have a reputation of excelling, often setting the standard very high for the TCK population. This is a benefit of growing up as a TCK and often results in college scholarships, mastery of extracurricular activities, and a fantastic and admirable work ethic. Unfortunately, along with that comes the belief that perfection is the expected standard and mistakes are inexcusable. Some of this stems from the external pressure of being "on stage" from a young age and knowing that their performance as a TCK will be critiqued by onlookers from around the world, including those who financially support their parent's job or ministry. Subpar is not acceptable, and failure is absolutely not an option. They have been taught that their actions have direct repercussions on others and that some of those consequences could be as severe as a parent's job loss or relocation. This pressure, though it may originate from external factors, becomes an internal battle that many TCKs deal with throughout their lifetimes. They succeed, and they are praised. Consequently, they equate the praise with academic and/or social success, which leads to the belief that their outstanding performance is the reason they are loved and accepted. Or they are propelled by the fear that their imperfection will reflect poorly on their parents, their parents' sending organization or business, their passport country, and (particularly for missionary kids) even God. Perfection is not optional, and failure becomes a tragedy. As you can imagine, this places a considerable amount of pressure on TCKs.

The Child Mind Institute says, "Not learning to tolerate failure leaves kids vulnerable to anxiety. It leads to meltdowns when the inevitable failure does occur, whether it happens in preschool or college. And perhaps even more important, it can make kids give up trying—or trying new things."[59]

TCKs are significantly more likely to experience high levels of anxiety than non-TCKs, and this often emerges from the internal and external pressure to excel and be above average.[60] As you raise your TCKs, it is critical to foster in them the knowledge that "failure is not fatal" so that they can develop a healthy balance of striving for excellence without being devastated by life's inevitable failures.

Here are some ways to go about combatting this expectation of unrealistic success:

Absolutely encourage excellence, but also reward your TCKs for their effort, no matter the outcome. If you can see that they are working diligently to master a concept, applaud them for trying whether or not they perfect it. No one can earn a perfect score in every area of life, and it is critical that your TCKs know that this is not your expectation. Your expectation should be that they try again, work hard, and don't give up when something doesn't come easily, but your expectation should not be perfection, and this needs to be verbally reiterated to your TCKs.

Model how to handle the disappointment of failure appropriately. Share with your kids when you have failed or have made a mistake to teach them that missteps are a natural part of life. They are watching your reactions, so be careful to react in a way that you would want them to repeat. Do not use negative self talk ("I'm so dumb!" "I really should be better at that." "I'm an idiot."), physically harm yourself or property (smacking the table or your leg, hitting your head against something, etc.), or blame others or the situation ("If it wasn't for _____, this wouldn't have happened." "I told him I didn't want to take this project on; if only he had listened.")

Empathize. When your TCKs inevitably make a mistake, acknowledge the negative feelings that accompany it. You can say, "I see that you are awfully disappointed. I'm sorry you are feeling that way." Gently remind them that mistakes are great learning experiences and that they can try again, but don't dismiss the negative feelings that come with failure.

Praise character over performance. Acknowledge and verbally uplift your children's unique qualities *whether or not they make mistakes*. If one of your children fails a test, say, "That must be so disappointing for you that you failed that test. You are such a smart kid, though, and I loved seeing your determination to do well. Let's see if we can help you be more prepared for the next one." Remind them that they are smart, funny, kind, good at building things, a great dancer, great at science, etc. and reiterate that making a mistake in those areas does not negate those qualities. They can still be a great dancer even if they made a mistake during the recital; they can still be great at science even if they fail their science test. When they fail is when they most need your encouragement to combat the negative voices in their heads telling them that they aren't good enough, smart enough, etc. Reiterate that physical ability is not the ultimate measure of acceptance and success but that their character is far more important. Praise their perseverance, insight, empathy, integrity twice as often as you praise their performance.

Balance change and acceptance. Teach your TCKs to accept that "what's done is done," and then work together to find things that they can change to yield a higher chance for success the next time. Failure is a great opportunity to find a better way to do something. Teach your TCKs to tolerate the frustration of failure and not to become paralyzed by anxiety, but instead to find ways to learn from it.

Let them fail. In order to learn to move on from mistakes and failures, TCKs need to be given the space to fail in a safe environment. This is not something that is enjoyable for any parent, but it is important that children experience failure so that they can learn to move forward after a mistake has been made. TCKs are less likely to be allowed the opportunity to misstep because of the unique pressures that the expatriate life brings for the family. Create a safe home environment where your TCKs can fail, and see that your love and support do not increase or decrease on the basis of their performance.

Like many common TCK trends, the TCK's desire both to succeed and to excel can be very positive and can lead to many opportunities. However, it must be accompanied by a healthy balance of tolerating, and not being devastated by, the inevitable failures that life brings. Learning to do this from a young age will be invaluable for your TCKs as they live overseas, navigate transitions between countries, and eventually grow up and live outside your home.

RELATED BENEFITS — CONTENTMENT:

TCKs who have realistic expectations of themselves and of life are more likely to be well-adjusted and happy adults. They are able to look back on their TCK lives as a fundamental part of their upbringing without being surprised and disappointed that they cannot recreate it as an adult. They become content and happy with the lives they are living when they have brought to light and processed the hidden expectations of how life is "supposed to go." They are able to enjoy the present and look forward into the future instead of being preoccupied with their past and thus appreciate their past experiences for what they offered and enjoy their current lives for what they are.

THE MAIN IDEAS:

- The TCK life can yield interesting expectations of what life "should" look like. If this isn't addressed and talked about, it can contribute to dissatisfaction and unsettledness in adulthood.
- There are often very high standards for TCKs because of their visible life. This can cause an extreme fear of failure, and it is important that this is combatted by praising character over performance and giving them space to fail.
- When TCKs are given space to make mistakes in their developmental years, they are more likely to give themselves grace when they do so in adulthood, as opposed to perceiving that any mistake is tragic.

QUESTIONS TO CONSIDER:

- How do you talk with your TCKs about their overseas upbringing? What message does this communicate to them?
- What are your expectations for their personal success and achievement? Are they influenced by your position/job as an expat? Does it allow them space to fail?
- How can you begin talking about their future and bring out their subconscious expectations?

CHAPTER 13

Maximizing the Benefits of the TCK Life

Healthy TCKs have recognized and processed the challenges of their unique upbringing and live out the benefits in their own life, recognizing that they are directly attributed to, and are often a product of, their TCK experience.

As I hope you have noticed as you have read the "Related Benefits" sections in each chapter, there are an incredible number of benefits that are unique to the TCK life. The experience of growing up cross-culturally truly prepares TCKs to be incredible members of our world, and when healthy, TCKs can bring about great change and lead cultures and societies in positive directions.

As you are intentional about caring for the challenges that TCKs face, it is equally as important that you encourage their superpowers. These beneficial skills are often directly tied to the challenges, and thus, it is important that they grow up hearing about the benefits as much as the challenges and how they often intertwine. Young adult TCKs who are struggling with the manifestations of TCK challenges will often clump the entire TCK experience into a negative category. While we can't deny its difficulties, I pray that they—because of your intentionality—can distinguish and appreciate how many

213

positive elements there are to their unique upbringing.

ADAPTABILITY, HOPE, AND RESILIENCE

One of the primary skills that TCKs are given credit for is their incredible adaptability—that is, the ability to adjust and change in order to fit within new conditions. This skill is one that can only be learned through practice, and TCKs typically have plenty of it.

Aside from the obvious pros of being able to adjust to new cultures, work environments, and social groups, adaptability has an additional advantage. Adaptability is a strong predictor of resilience. Dean Becker, president and CEO of a company that creates programs to teach resiliency, believes adaptability is a trait that is a key determinant of an individual's success. When individuals can adjust to a variety of environments and circumstances and find contentment in them, they are much more likely to be healthy and stable individuals. I have seen a particular ability in adult TCKs to live through unfamiliar or difficult circumstances yet remain emotionally stable, strong, and optimistic.

While it is difficult to watch the development of resiliency in your children through the challenging seasons that they go through as TCKs, it is through these challenges that they learn how to adapt and be flexible. When they do so successfully, they develop resilience – "the process of adapting well in the face of adversity, trauma, tragedy, threats or significant sources of stress. It means "bouncing back" from difficult experiences."[61] We all know that life can be difficult, so the fact that TCKs have been armed with resiliency as the result of their adaptability is a gift that will serve them well.

A study done in 1999 identified four contributing factors in the development of resiliency: social competence, problem solving skills, autonomy, and a sense of purpose. By caring for your TCK well, they can develop these attributes and thus, develop resiliency – an overarching benefit of the TCK experience.[62]

Adaptability is also a valuable, sought-after skill in the workplace. The *Harvard Business Review* published an article titled "Adaptability: The New Competitive Advantage."[63] The article discusses the vital trait of adaptability in leaders, employers, businesses, and employees in our globalizing world. Third Culture Kids naturally have this "new competitive advantage," which will be an incredible asset to them when they one day have careers. It is also an incredible asset to society as we are, more than ever, needing more adaptable people in the increasingly culturally diverse workplace. In another article about TCKs in leadership, their ability to adapt creates, "a stronger and more robust mental focus, which enables individuals to cope better with change and empower others to do the same. As leaders, this demographic is able to empathize with the negative impacts of change and manage these in a way that helps those who are struggling."[64]

Encourage your TCKs' adaptability by praising this as a valuable skill. Many TCKs are not told until adulthood, often by their employers, that their level of adaptability is rare and treasured. When they are aware that this is a skill they possess, they can use it as a point of confidence during future transitions, job interviews, life challenges, and so many other areas where this trait has immeasurable value.

By pointing out your TCKs' adaptability, you are also balancing out the sometimes negative-sounding talk of their restlessness. While this restlessness, as we discussed in chapter 10, is an issue that needs to be addressed, it is also important to spend time talking about the benefit associated with restlessness. In other words, while it is and will be difficult to learn how to manage their need for change—especially in adulthood—the reward of doing so is the ability to be stable yet also incredibly adaptable within their environment.

GLOBAL CITIZENRY

For many TCKs, their favorite part of the Olympics is when the athletes without a country (independents) march through the processional. There is a sense of "Those are my people!" They can identify with the feeling of not having a particular country that they represent and not feeling like they could possibly choose a single flag to display. They simply feel too connected to too many places to choose a favorite.

It is important that you appreciate this about them and encourage their global citizenship. It is a trait that will not only serve them well personally but also is such an incredible asset to our increasingly interconnected world. I think it would be to the world's advantage to have more TCKs in leadership positions at every level, and the primary reason is this: TCKs have an appreciation for the world as a whole more than possibly any other single people group. They aren't typically loyal to one place, and thus, they can love and appreciate many places and people without being influenced by stigmas, stereotypes, and prejudices that develop when you have an "us versus them" mentality. TCKs are good at looking at the world from an "us" perspective, and this is an attribute that you should praise in your TCKs as opposed to being concerned about a lack of patriotism.

Encourage them to read the global news, get involved in micro-politics, cheer for any sports team no matter the country, and not need to choose favorites. Before long, people will be looking to your global citizens for direction in how to navigate a globalized world.

CONFIDENCE IN THEIR BEAUTIFULLY COMPLEX IDENTITY

As we looked at, there are so many elements that make up the TCK identity. For a while, it is confusing for TCKs to sort out how these puzzle pieces fit together, but, when they do, it is one of my favorite things to watch. They become confident individuals who have so many interesting layers to who they are and how they came to be that way. They learn to love and appreciate all aspects of who they are and how they were influenced by their overseas upbringing and other experiences.

I have seen that adult TCKs tend to take a drastic leap from being incredibly self-conscious and unsure about who they are, to being incredibly self-confident and proud of who they are. The age that this takes place is different for every TCK, but when it does happen, it is incredible. They finally feel comfortable in their skin enough to not constantly use their chameleon powers and they exude all of the amazing TCK benefits we have discussed. Their beautifully complex identity no longer feels like a liability but can finally be appreciated for the amazing asset that it is.

HIGH ACHIEVERS

Third Culture Kids are extremely high achievers. When I lived overseas, it was not uncommon for classmates to have exceptionally high SAT and ACT scores that resulted in American universities offering full-ride scholarships that included a stipend to visit family back in Africa each summer. Many others were masters of their sport, art, or craft. In those circles, it was abnormal to be mediocre. This high-achieving status affords TCKs many opportunities and further demonstrates how, combined with an amazing adaptability and global perspective, they can truly be world changers.

As I discussed in chapter 12, there is a fine balance between encouraging success and also allowing for mistakes and failures. As you seek to maximize the benefits of their high-achieving nature, there are 2 things to keep in mind:

1. The best way to maximize the benefit of being a high achiever is to teach them how to recover from failures and mistakes. Mistakes are inevitable, and for a TCK who didn't learn that, a mistake can be devastating and debilitating.

2. For most TCKs, the high-achieving status comes naturally because of the community around them. When the standard is high for other expatriate children, most often they will all more or less measure up to that standard. Therefore, my encouragement is to not worry about putting effort into maximizing this wonderful TCK trait. Yes, encourage hard work, discipline, and diligence, but don't fret about ensuring that your TCK becomes one of these high achievers—they most likely will.

EMPATHY

"Empathy is the state of feeling into another person's reality."[65]

Because TCKs have the ability to see things from many different perspectives, they also have the ability to feel into another person's reality on a greater level than people who have only lived in one culture. This skill of empathy correlates directly with great listening skills, conflict resolution, and communication abilities. The unique piece of TCK empathy specifically, is that they are able to utilize these skills across cultural differences. They have learned to not only see things from different perspectives but also to empathize with people whose life experiences are very different from their own.

Empathy also helps TCKs to learn how to enter into deep relationships. They can capitalize on their empathetic nature as a way to connect with people on a heart-level and, if they let themselves, they can develop long-lasting friendships using this as a means of lowering barriers.

EMOTIONAL AWARENESS THAT LEAVES AN EMOTIONALLY HEALTHY LEGACY

"Emotional Intelligence (EQ) is the ability to identify, use, understand, and manage emotions in an effective and positive way."[66] TCKs have a unique opportunity to learn how to be very emotionally aware individuals. Because their young lives often include many transitions, challenges, and conflicts, there are many occasions during which they can learn how to "identify, use, understand, and manage" feelings if they are taught how to do this.

It may feel like talking about feelings and emotions and many of the ideas discussed in chapter 2 is unnecessary and uncomfortable, but I assure you these emotions and struggles are a gateway to unleashing this TCK superpower. As you implement the practices throughout this book, please be vigilant about helping your children to learn to name and manage their emotions. Do this through your conversations, your own modeling, and your clear intentionality that shows them that this type of expression is an important life skill.

Emotional health is one trait that is nearly guaranteed to pass down to the next generation because parents can't help but implement it as they raise their own children. By being intentional about being emotionally healthy yourself and raising emotionally healthy children, you are setting your grandchildren up for emotional health as well. You are leaving a legacy by raising up a healthy Third Culture Kid.

Final Thoughts

I would not be writing this book had it not been for my TCK experience in all of its benefits and challenges. I wouldn't be able to look a teenage TCK in the eye and say, "I know this is so hard. I have been there. I understand." I wouldn't be able to say to parents that moving overseas with children is so worth it, despite the difficulties. These things have only arisen from coming face to face with the ampersand nature of the TCK life. From the realization that in the soil of the challenges is where my most quality traits were planted, waiting to be nourished by wonderful souls who would pour in love and understanding. My experience as a Third Culture Kid mirrors the experiences of hundreds of others with whom I have worked.

As you love, support, and raise up Third Culture Kids, I pray that you become that person who pours into their life with wisdom and understanding of the particular challenges they are up against, and prepared with a proactive approach to come alongside them. I pray that through your loving, preventive care, your TCKs thrive as whole, healthy, and uniquely beautiful individuals who love their ampersand life.

ABOUT TCK TRAINING

TCK Training began as a blog back in 2016. At that time, I was the TCK Program Director for CultureBound and using curriculum that I developed to prepare TCKs-to-be to learn a new culture and language. I taught the children and teens and had one 1-hour session with the parents. There was no way I could even scratch the surface of what I felt these parents needed to know in such a short time. It wasn't uncommon for that session to be continued through the lunch break and for parents to ask for a dinner conversation to continue talking about TCK care. After doing that for 2 years, I started the TCK Training blog as a way to continue the conversation for those parents. I wanted to provide practical ways for them to be intentional about every step of raising their TCKs. I found that the blog also became a way for me to process my own TCK-life. Up until that point, I had never considered myself a writer and certainly never anticipated writing a book, but through four years of blogging, I developed a love for typing out my thoughts and I heard over and over how helpful and unique my practical, preventive approach was.

Over the years, TCK Training has grown from a simple blog to an organization that provides many resources around the concept of practical, preventive care for TCKs.

Some of these services are:

Live Workshops: These are offered every few months and are so fun. They take place online and include teaching, discussion, giveaways, and are a great way to develop a deep understanding of preventive TCK care and to get to know others who work with and/or parent TCKs.

Seminars: Seminars are online videos that are less than one hour long and go deep with one topic. For example: Preventing and Resolving Unresolved Grief. I post a new seminar each month.

Coaching for Parents: This is one of my very favorite things to do. Through coaching, I help parents to troubleshoot common challenges of moving and/or raising kids overseas in ways that are specific to their family's needs and children's personalities.

Consulting for Organizations: I have found that many organizations that offer TCK programs often benefit tremendously from learning how to tweak their program to be more preventive-care focus. I look at what they are already doing with their TCK program and help them to modify it to encourage a more preventive approach.

Teaching and Training Teachers: I am available to teach at TCK retreats and programs and/or to train staff members to teach TCKs. This includes curriculum creation for these events.

Speaking Events: I am available for speaking events and workshops on various topics specific to TCK Care.

For more information about these services
and to stay informed about what
TCK Training is doing visit

www.TCKTraining.com

NOTES

[1] David C. Pollock, Ruth E. Van Reken, and Michael V. Pollock, *Third Culture Kids 3rd Edition: Growing Up Among Worlds* (London: Nicholas Brealey, 2017), 43.

[2] Pollock, Van Reken and Pollock, 27.

[3] United Nations, "The Number of International Migrants Reaches 272 Million, Continuing an Upward Trend in All World Regions, Says UN," UN.org, September 17, 2019, https://www.un.org/development/desa/en/news/population/international-migrant-stock-2019.html.

[4] Ted Ward, "The MK's Advantage: Three Cultural Contexts," in Pam Echerd and Alice Arathoon, eds., *Understanding and Nurturing the Missionary Family: Compendium of the International Conference on Missionary Kids Quito Ecuador January 4–8, 1987* (Pasadena, CA: William Carey Library, 1989), 49–61.

[5] Lois J. Bushong, *Belonging Everywhere and Nowhere: Insights into Counseling the Globally Mobile* (Indianapolis, IN: Mango Tree Intercultural Services, 2013), 10.

[6] Tanya Crossman, *Misunderstood: The Impact of Growing Up Overseas in the 21st Century* (United Kingdom: Summertime, 2016), 34.

[7] F. M. Alpass and S. Neville, "Loneliness, Health and Depression in Older Males," *Aging & Mental Health* 7, no. 3 (2003): 212–16, https://doi.org/10.1080/1360786031000101193.

[8] Ruth Hill Useem and Ann Baker Cottrell, "TCKs Four Times More Likely to Earn Bachelor's Degrees," *NewsLinks – The Newspaper of International Schools Services* 12, no. 5 (May 1993): http://www.tckworld.com/useem/art2.html.

[9] Middle three statistics on this list can be found in the following source: Sean D. Truman, David A. Sharar, and John C. Pompe, "The Mental Health Status of Expatriate Versus U.S. Domestic Workers," *International Journal of Mental Health* 40, no. 4 (January 2011): 3-18, https://doi.org/10.2753/IMH0020-7411400401.

[10] More research statistics can be found at www.TCKidnow.com.

[11] Kelli Harding, *The Rabbit Effect: Live Longer, Happier, and Healthier with the Groundbreaking Science of Kindness* (New York: Atria Books, 2019), 134.

[12] Kelli Harding, *The Rabbit Effect: Live Longer, Happier, and Healthier with the Groundbreaking Science of Kindness* (New York: Atria Books, 2019), 193.

[13] V. J. Felitti, R. F. Anda, D. Nordenberg, D. F. Williamson, A. M. Spitz, V. Edwards, M. P. Koss, and J. S. Marks, "Relationship of Childhood Abuse and Household Dysfunction to Many of the

Leading Causes of Death in Adults: The Adverse Childhood Experiences (ACE) Study, *American Journal of Preventive Medicine* 14 (1998): 245–58.

[14] *The Rabbit Effect*, 192.

[15] Brené Brown, *Daring Greatly: How the Courage to be Vulnerable Transforms the Way We Live, Love, Parent, and Lead* (New York: Avery, 2012), 216.

[16] Joshua Straub, *Safe House: How Emotional Safety Is the Key to Raising Kids Who Live, Love, and Lead Well* (Colorado Spring, CO: WaterBrook, 2015), 29.

[17] Diann M. Ackard et al., "Parent-Child Connectedness and Behavioral and Emotional Health Among Adolescents," *American Journal of Preventive Medicine* 30, no. 1 (January 2006): 59–66, https://doi.org/10.1016/j.amepre.2005.09.013.

[18] Joshua Straub, *Safe House: How Emotional Safety Is the Key to Raising Kids Who Live, Love, and Lead Well* (Colorado Spring, CO: WaterBrook, 2015), 28.

[19] Joshua Straub, *Safe House: How Emotional Safety Is the Key to Raising Kids Who Live, Love, and Lead Well* (Colorado Spring, CO: WaterBrook, 2015), 28.

[20] Joshua Straub, 28.

[21] Joshua Straub, 17.

[22] Daniel J. Siegel and Tina Payne Bryson, "Discipline: It's All About Connection," *Work and Family Life Journal* 30, no. 4 (April 2015): 2.

[23] Joshua Straub, 44.

[24] "What Is Emotional Intelligence?," www.PsychologyToday.com, accessed January 9, 2020, https://www.psychologytoday.com/intl/basics/emotional-intelligence.

[25] David C. Pollock, Ruth E. Van Reken, and Michael V. Pollock, *Third Culture Kids 3rd Edition: Growing Up Among Worlds* (London: Nicholas Brealey, 2017), 240.

[26] Danielle Kaufman, "The Importance of Routine in Childhood," accessed March 2019, Melbourne Child Psychology & School Psychology Services, Port Melbourne, https://www.melbournechildpsychology.com.au/blog/the-importance-of-routine-in-childhood/.

[27] Brené Brown, *Daring Greatly: How the Courage to be Vulnerable Transforms the Way We Live, Love, Parent, and Lead* (New York: Avery, 2012), 240.

[28] David C. Pollock, Ruth E. Van Reken, and Michael V. Pollock, *Third Culture Kids 3rd Edition: Growing Up Among Worlds* (London: Nicholas Brealey, 2017), 87-91.

[29] David C. Pollock, Ruth E. Van Reken, and Michael V. Pollock, 91

[30] Brené Brown, *The Gifts of Imperfection: Let Go of Who You Think You're Supposed to Be and Embrace Who You Are* (Minnesota: Hazelden, 2010), 64.

[31] Tanya Crossman, *Misunderstood: The Impact of Growing Up Overseas in the 21st Century* (United Kingdom: Summertime, 2016), 153.

[32] Out of the Fog, *Complex Post Traumatic Stress Disorder* (C-PTSD) n.d. https://outofthefog.website/toolbox-1/2015/11/17/ complex-post-traumatic-stress-disorder-c-ptsd

[33] Lois Busong, *Depression and Third Culture Kids*, August 17, 2014, https://www.loisbushong.com/posts/2018/1/9/ depression-and-third-culture-kids

[34] Belinda Bauman, *Brave Souls: Experiencing the Audacious Power of Empathy* (Downers Grove, IL: IVP Books, 2019), 9.

[35] Elyssa Barbash, "Different Types of Trauma: Small 't' versus Large 'T'," www.PsychologyToday.com, published March 3, 2017, https:// www.psychologytoday.com/us/blog/trauma-and-hope/201703/ different-types-trauma-small-t-versus-large-t.

[36] Elyssa Barbash.

[37] Chris Cortman and Joseph Walden, *Keep Pain in the Past: Getting Over Trauma, Grief and the Worst That's Ever Happened to You,* (Coral Gables, FL: Mango, 2018).

[38] Cissy White, "Putting Resilience and Resilience Surveys Under the Microscope," ACEs Connection, published February 6, 2017, https://www.acesconnection.com/blog/putting-resilience-and-resilience-surveys-under-the-microscope?reply=465321300828496842.

[39] C. E. Agaibi and J. P. Wilson, "Trauma, PTSD, and Resilience: A Review of the Literature," *Trauma, Violence, & Abuse* 6, no. 3 (July 2005): 195–216, https://doi.org/10.1177/1524838005277438.

[40] Brené Brown, *Daring Greatly: How the Courage to be Vulnerable Transforms the Way We Live, Love, Parent, and Lead* (New York: Avery, 2012), 107.

[41] Brené Brown, D*aring Greatly: How the Courage to be Vulnerable Transforms the Way We Live, Love, Parent, and Lead* (New York: Avery, 2012), 232.

[42] Bruce Feiler, "The Stories that Bind Us" The New York Times, published March 15, 2013, https://www.nytimes.com/2013/03/17/fashion/the-family-stories-that-bind-us-this-life.html

[43] Meg Meeker, *Parenting Great Kids Podcast*, Setting Boundaries with Kids (with guest Dr. Henry Cloud), Episode 76. (2018).

[44] Brooker, Liz and Woodhead, Martin eds. (2008). *Developing Positive Identities: Diversity and Young Children.* Early Childhood in Focus (3). Milton Keynes: Open University.

[45] Bruce Feiler, "The Stories that Bind Us" The New York Times, published March 15, 2013, https://www.nytimes.com/2013/03/17/fashion/the-family-stories-that-bind-us-this-life.html

[46] The Family Dinner Project, "Benefits of Family Dinners, 2020, https://thefamilydinnerproject.org/about-us/benefits-of-family-dinners/

[47] David C. Pollock, Ruth E. Van Reken, and Michael V. Pollock, *Third Culture Kids 3rd Edition: Growing Up Among Worlds* (London: Nicholas Brealey, 2017), 15-33.

[48] David C. Pollock, Ruth E. Van Reken, and Michael V. Pollock, 25.

[49] Julien Borrelle, *Ted Talk*, Learn a New Culture, (2017) https://www.youtube.com/watch?v=GhA9eypocE0

[50] Laurie Vasquez, "The Sooner You Expose a Baby to a Second Language, the Smarter They'll Be," www.BigThink.com, published April 8, 2016, https://bigthink.com/laurie-vasquez/the-sooner-you-expose-a-baby-to-a-second-language-the-smarter-theyll-be?utm_medium=Social&utm_source=Facebook&fbclid=IwAR0jbv55NBToPLctaQ6ZEYaaPg841Ddsyt9JGzE0LdlXVS-ucwkpSodVyx0#Echobox=1575747895.

[51] "Parlez-Vous Français? The Advantages of Bilingualism in Canada," Canadian Council on Learning: Lessons in Learning, published October 16, 2008, accessed January 16, 2020, http://elearning.wqsb.qc.ca/eAccounting/Module_11/documents/The-advantages-of-bilingualism-how%20important%20it%20is.pdf.

[52] Aneurin Howorth, "A TCK's Struggle with Depression – Guest Post," www.TCKTraining.com, published April 5, 2018, https://www.tcktraining.com/blog/a-tcks-struggle-with-depression-guest-post?rq=depression.

[53] R. A. Hill and R. I. Dunbar, "Social Network Size in Humans," *Human Nature* 14 (March 2003): 53, https://doi.org/10.1007/s12110-003-1016-y.

[54] UHBLOG, "The Top 5 Most Stressful Life Events and How to Handle Them," University Hospitals, UHHospitals.org, published July 2 2015, https://www.uhhospitals.org/Healthy-at-UH/articles/2015/07/the-top-5-most-stressful-life-events.

[55] Elaina Natario, "INFOGRAPHIC: The Modern Third Culture Kid," published September 2011, https://denizenmag.com/2011/09/infographic-the-modern-third-culture-kid/.

[56] Marilyn Gardner, *Between Worlds: Essays on Culture and Belonging* (Doorlight Publications, 2014), 38.

57 Guy Winch, *Emotional First Aid: Practical Strategies for Treating Failure, Rejection, Guilt and Other Everyday Psychological Injuries* (New York: Penguin Group, 2014)

58 Brené Brown, *Daring Greatly: How the Courage to be Vulnerable Transforms the Way We Live, Love, Parent, and Lead* (New York: Avery, 2012), 14.

59 Beth Arky, "How to Help Kids Learn to Fail: Only Through Trial and Error Can Children Become Resillient Adults," Child Mind Institute, https://childmind.org/article/how-to-help-kids-learn-to-fail/.

60 Tanya Crossman, *Misunderstood: The Impact of Growing Up Overseas in the 21st Century* (United Kingdom: Summertime, 2016), 282.

61 "The Road to Resilience," American Psychological Association, accessed February 9, 2020, https://www.apa.org/helpcenter/road-resilience.

62 Martin L. Krovetz, "Resiliency: A Key Element for Supporting Youth At-Risk," The Clearing House: A Journal of Educational Strategies, Issues and Ideas 73, no. 2 (1999): 121–123, DOI: 10.1080/00098659909600163.

63 Martin Reeves and Mike Deimler, "Adaptability: The New Competitive Advantage," *Harvard Business Review* (July-August 2011), https://hbr.org/2011/07/

adaptability-the-new-competitive-advantage.

[64] Lewis Humphries, "8 Reasons Third Culture Kids Have the Potential to Be Great Leaders," LifeHack.org, accessed February 9, 2020, https://www.lifehack.org/articles/productivity/8-reasons-third-culture-kids-have-the-potential-great-leaders.html.

[65] Belinda Bauman, *Brave Souls: Experiencing the Audacious Power of Empathy* (Downers Grove, IL: IVP Books, 2019), 40.

[66] Paula Durlofsky, "The Benefits of Emotional Intelligence," www.PsychCentral.com, updated July 8, 2018, https://psychcentral.com/blog/the-benefits-of-emotional-intelligence/.